TABLECLOTHS

M000113692

1

Instructions on page 17

Instructions on page 19

Instructions on page 20

3

Instructions on page 111

Instructions on page 30

Instructions on page 21

Instructions on page 108

Instructions on page 114

Instructions on page 23

Instructions on page 25

10

Instructions on page 26

Instructions on page 27

Instructions on page 28

Instructions on page 29

Instructions on page 108

1 Tablecloth

shown on page 1

You'll Need:
Crochet cotton DMC #3, 248 20-g. balls White. Steel crochet hook size 1.75 mm. 172 plastic rings 2 cm in diameter.

Finished Size: 170 cm in diameter
Size of Motif: 8.5 cm in diameter
Gauge: 1 row of dc = 0.9 cm
Making Instructions:
Motif: Ch 12, sl st in 1st st to form ring.
Rnd 1: Ch 3, 23 dc in ring, sl st in 3rd st of beg ch.
Rnd 2: Ch 4, 1 tr, (ch 4, 2 tr at a time) 11 times, ch 4, sl st in 1st tr.
Rnd 3: 1 sl st, ch 3, work "1 dc, ch 5, 2 dc" in lp, (work "2 dc, ch 5, 2 dc" in next lp) 11 times, sl st in 3rd st of beg ch.
Rnd 4: Ch 1, * 1 sc, work "1 sc, 1 hdc, 5dc, 1 hdc, 1 sc" in lp, sk 1 dc, 1 sc, repeat from * 12 times, end sl st in 1st st of beg ch. From 2nd motif, work middle dc of each petal joining to adjacent motif. Join 7 motifs round.

Pattern crochet: Rnd 1: Join cotton in motif, ch 12 (1 dc, ch 9 from next), 1 dc in the middle of next petal, ch 9, work 4 dtr at a time drawing through 2 places each of next petal and the petal of adjacent motif, ch 9, continue in same manner around.
Rnd 2: Ch 1, 1 sc, * 11 sc in ch-9, sc in sc, repeat from * around, end ch 9, sl st in 1st ch.
Rnd 3: Ch 5, sk 2 sc, dc in sc, * ch 2, sk 2 sc, dc in sc, repeat from * around, end sl st in 3rd st of beg ch.
Rnd 4: 1 sl st, ch 3, work "1 dc, ch 2, 2 dc" in ch-2, ch 6, * sk 2 sps, "2 dc, ch 2, 2 dc, ch 6" (shell st), repeat from * around, end sl st in 3rd st of beg ch.
Rnd 5: Stitch as for rnd 4, working "ch 2, sc in ch-6, ch 2" between shell sts.
Rnd 6: Work "ch 3, 1 sc, ch 3" between shell sts.
Rnds 7-9: Work as for rnds 4-6, following to the number of ch indicated. End ch 3, 1 tr instead of ch 7.
Rnd 10: Ch 9, 1 sc, continue in same way as for rnd 1.
Rnd 11: 10 sc each in 1st and 2nd lp, 11 sc each in following lps.

(Continued on Next Page)

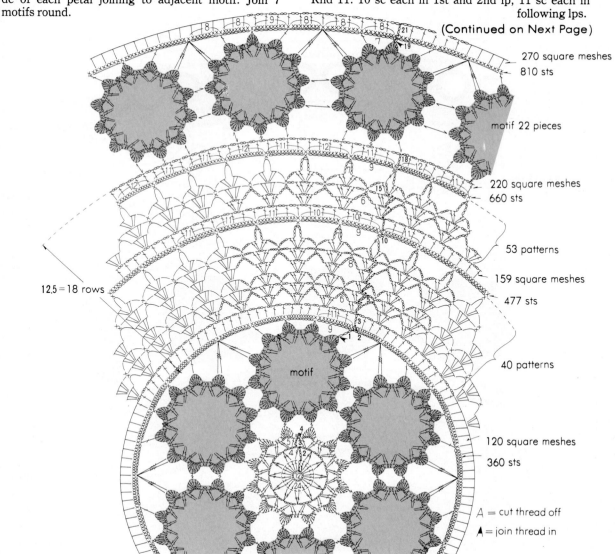

270 square meshes
810 sts

motif 22 pieces

220 square meshes
660 sts

53 patterns

159 square meshes

477 sts

40 patterns

12.5 = 18 rows

motif

120 square meshes
360 sts

A = cut thread off

A = join thread in

17

Rnds 12-14: Work same way as for rnds 3-5.
Rnds 15-16: Work as for rnds 9-10.
Rnd 17: Work as for rnd 11, following to the number of sc indicated.
Rnd 18: Work as for rnd 3.
Having worked rnd 18, work 22 motifs around.
Rnds 19-36: Join in new cotton, work pattern crochet up to rnd 36 as for rnds 1-18, join 38 motifs around.
Rnds 37-51: Work as for rnds 19-36.
Join cotton to plastic ring, work 15 sc each in 172 rings, wrapping half the circle of each ring. Work 15 sc each in half the circles remained, end sl st in 1st st.
Rnds 52-66: Work as for rnds 10-18. Work 70 motifs around.

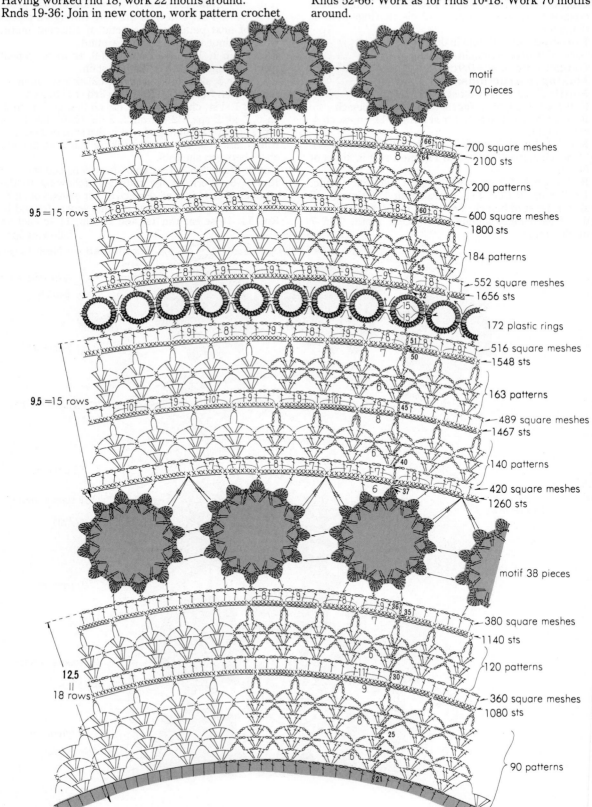

motif
70 pieces

700 square meshes
2100 sts

200 patterns

600 square meshes
1800 sts

184 patterns

552 square meshes
1656 sts

172 plastic rings

516 square meshes
1548 sts

163 patterns

489 square meshes
1467 sts

140 patterns

420 square meshes
1260 sts

motif 38 pieces

380 square meshes
1140 sts

120 patterns

360 square meshes
1080 sts

90 patterns

9.5 =15 rows

9.5 =15 rows

12.5
=
18 rows

2 Tablecloth shown on page 2

You'll Need:
Crochet cotton DMC #5, 64 20-g. balls White. Steel crochet hook size 1.50 mm.
Finished Size: 187 cm by 132 cm
Size of Motif: A = 11 cm in diameter.
Gauge: 3 rows of dc = 2 cm
Making Instructions:
A-motif: Ch 7, sl st in 1st ch to form ring.
Rnd 1: Ch 1, 16 sc in ring, sl st in 1st ch.
Rnd 2: Ch 4, (dc in sc, ch 1) 15 times, sl st in 3rd st of beg ch.
Rnd 3: 1 sl st, ch 5, * dc in ch, ch 2, repeat from * around, sl st in 3rd st of beg ch.
Rnd 4: Ch 1, sc in ch, * ch 6, 1 dc each in 5th and 6th ch from hook, sc in next dc previous rnd, repeat from * around, end 1 dc each in 2 ch, sl st in 1st ch.
Rnd 5: Sl st in 4 sts, * sc in ch, ch 4, repeat from * around, sl st in 1st sc.

Rnd 6: Ch 3, * 4 dc in lp, 1 dc in next sc, repeat from * around, sl st in 3rd st of beg ch.
Rnd 7: 1 sl st between sts, ch 5, * sk 2 dc, 1 dc between sts next, ch 2, repeat from * around, sl st in 3rd st of beg ch.
Rnd 8: Ch 1, 1 sc, * ch 3, dc in dc, ch 3, sc in dc, ch 5, sc in same st as last sc, ch 3, sl st in same st as last sc, ch 3, sc in next dc, repeat from * around, sl st in 1st ch.
From 2nd motif, work middle p making sl st to join where indicated. Make 12 rows of 17 motifs.
B-motif: Ch 7, sl st in 1st ch to form ring.
Rnds 1-2: Work as for A-motif.
Rnd 3: Work as for rnd 8 of A-motif, joining to adjacent A.
Make 176 motifs.

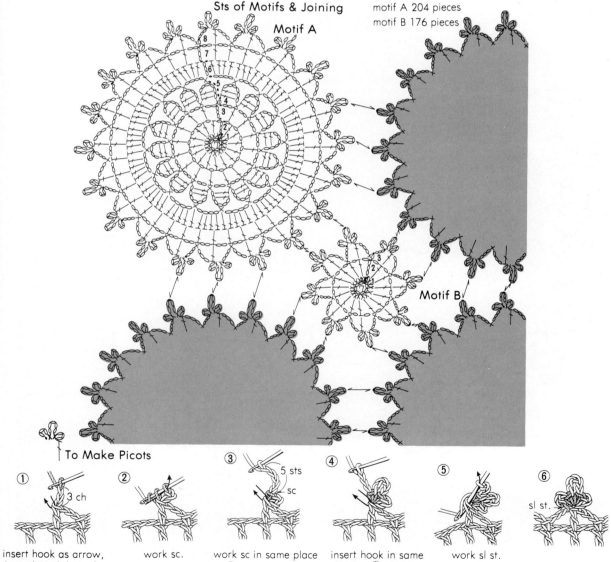

Sts of Motifs & Joining

Motif A

Motif B

motif A 204 pieces
motif B 176 pieces

To Make Picots

① 3 ch
insert hook as arrow, draw thread through.

② work sc.

③ 5 sts / sc
work sc in same place as ①.

④ insert hook in same place as ③.

⑤ work sl st.

⑥ sl st.

3 Tablecloth
shown on page 3

You'll Need:
Crochet cotton DMC #5, 91 20-g. balls White. Steel crochet hook size 1.50 mm.
Finished Size: 171 cm by 143.5 cm
Size of Motif: A = 22 cm in diameter B = 3 cm in diameter.
Gauge: 1 row of dc = 0.8 cm
Making Instructions:
A-motif: Ch 10, sl st in 1st st to form ring.
Rnd 1: Ch 3, 19 dc in ring, sl st in 3rd st of beg ch.
Rnd 2: Ch 6, * sk 1 dc, dc in dc, ch 3, repeat from * around, sl st in 3rd st of beg ch.

Rnd 3: Ch 1, * work "1 sc, 1 hdc, 2 dc, 1 hdc, 1 sc" in ch-3 lp, repeat from * around, sl st in 1st ch.
Rnd 4: Ch 1, * sc in wrong side of dc on rnd 2, ch 5, repeat from * around, end sl st in 1st ch.
Rnd 5: Sl st in lp, ch 1, * work "1 sc, 1 hdc, 5dc, 1 hdc, 1 sc" in lp, repeat from * around, end sl st in 1st ch.
Rnd 6: Sl st in each of 4 dc, ch 7, * work "1 hdc, ch 3, 1 hdc" in middle dc previous rnd, ch 5, repeat from * around, end 1 hdc, ch 3, sl st in 2nd st of beg ch.
Rnd 7: Sl st in ch-5 lp, ch 1, 6 sc in same lp as sl st, 4 sc in ch-3 lp, continue working 6 sc and 4 sc alternately around. End sl st in 1st ch.

unify lps on rnds 1-3 with sc on 4th rnd.
*work sc 4th rnd

A = join thread in

work sc on 4th rnd of
A-motif in wrong side
of dc 2nd rnd.

Edging

Motif A

Motif B

= work in ch previous rnd.

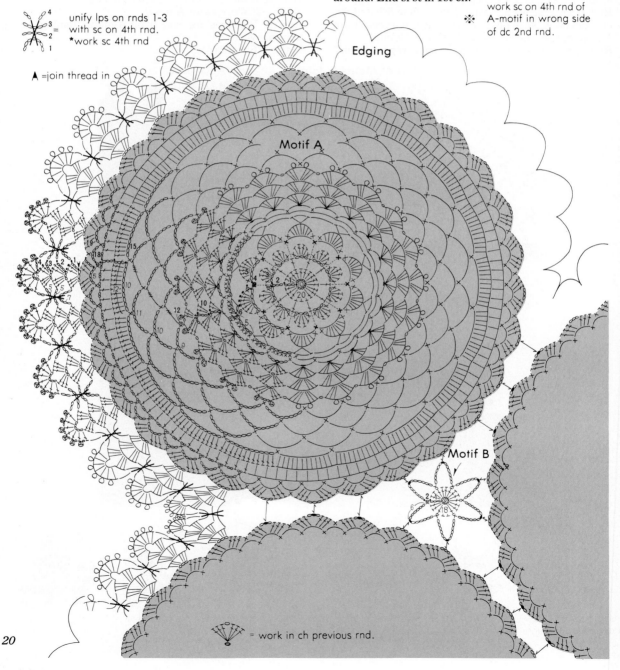

Rnd 8: Ch 1, 1 sc, * ch 5, sk 4 sc, sc in sc, repeat from * around, end ch 2, 1 dc, instead of ch 5.
Rnd 9: Ch 4, 3 dc in last dc previous rnd, * work "3 dc, ch 1, 3 dc" in middle st of ch-5, repeat from * around, end 2 dc, sl st in 3rd st of beg ch.
Rnd 10: Work as for previous rnd, making ch-3 between 2 of 3 dc.
Rnd 11: Sl st in 2 sts, ch 3, 3-ch p, 2 dc, ch 1, * work "3 dc, 3-ch p, ch 3, 3-ch p, 3 dc, ch 1" in ch-3, repeat from * around, end ch 1, 1 hdc, instead of ch 3.
Rnd 12: Ch 1, 1 sc, * ch 9, 1 sc, repeat from * around, end ch 4, 1 dtr.
Rnds 13-14: Work as for rnd 12, increasing sts of ch.
Rnd 15: Work 1 sc, ch 10, alternately around.
Rnd 16: Sl st in ch, ch 3, 11 dc in lp, 12 dc in each lp around, end sl st in 3rd st of beg ch.
Rnd 17: Ch 5, * sk 1 dc, dc in dc, ch 2, repeat from * around, end sl st in 3rd st of beg ch.
Rnd 18: Sl st in ch, ch 1, * 1 sc in ch-2, ch 5, repeat from * around, sl st in 1st ch.
Rnd 19: Sl st in ch, ch 3, work "2 dc, ch 3, 3 dc" in lp, * sc in next lp, work "3 dc, ch 3, 3 dc" in lp followed, repeat from * around, end 1 sc, sl st in 3rd st of beg ch.
End off.
From 2nd motif, work rnd 19 joining to adjacent motifs as shown. Make 7 rows of 7 motifs.
B-motif: Ch 9, sl st in 1st ch to form ring.
Rnd 1: Ch 3, 17 dc in ring, sl st in 3rd st of beg ch.
Rnd 2: Ch 1, 1 sc, * ch 6, sl st to A-motif, ch 6, sk 2 dc, 1 dc, repeat from * around, sl st in 1st ch. End off.

Edging: Rnd 1: Join cotton in A-motif, work as for rnd 19, making ch-7 between patterns.
Rnds 2-3: Work as for rnd 1.
Rnd 4: Sl st in 3 sts, ch 3, 3-ch p, ch 1, (dc in lp, 3-ch p, ch 1) 5 times, dc in same lp as last st, ch 2, sc in the lp on 1st rnd wrapping lps 2nd and 3rd rnd together in the st. Continue in same manner around, end sl st in 3rd st of beg ch. End off.

Chart on Measurements   motif A 49 pieces
                         motif B 72 pieces

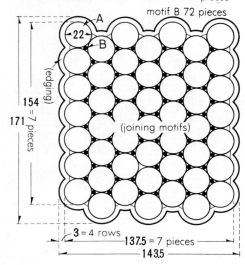

6 Tablecloth shown on page 6

You'll Need:
Crochet cotton DMC #3, 109 20-g. balls Ivory. Steel crochet hook size 1.75 mm.
Finished Size: 164 cm in diameter.
Gauge: 1 row of dc = 0.7 cm
Making Instructions:
Ch 12, sl st in 1st ch to form ring.
Rnd 1: Ch 1, 24 sc in ring, sl st in 1st ch.
Rnd 2: Ch 3, 2-dc puff in same place as ch-3, * ch 2, sk 1 sc, 3-dc puff, repeat from * around, sl st in 1st puff st.
Rnd 3: Ch 5, dc in same place as ch-5, ch 2, * work "1 dc, ch 2, 1 dc" in puff st, ch 2, repeat from * around, sl st in 3rd st of beg ch.
Rnd 4: Ch 5, work filet crochet (1 dc, ch 2) around, end sl st in 3rd st of beg ch.

Rnds 5-20: Work filet crochet (1 dc, ch 2) increasing sts at 6 places as shown.
Rnds 21-82: Work as for previous rnd, increasing sts at 6 places. Work 1 dc, ch 2, for each sp, 3 dc for each bl.
Rnds 83-84: Where at the place to increase, work dc as shown. Work 1 side each crossway from next rnd.

Beginning
of the Sts

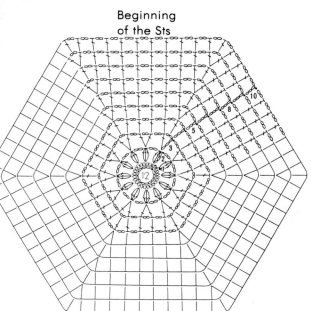

Chart on Measurements

42 = 53 square meshes
67 = 85 square meshes
23 = 32 rows
59 = 84 rows
82 = 116 rows

Rnd 85: Join new cotton in, ch 5, 7 dc, work filet crochet in the sts followed, end ch 2, 1 dc.

Rnds 86-94: Work straight as for rnd 85. Make 1 sp at the end of rnd 94, working 2 sts (dc and dtr) at a time.

Rnds 95-101: Work decreasing 1 sp each side. Work each end as for rnd 94.

Rnds 102-108: Work as for rnds 85-94.

Rnds 109-116: Work decreasing 1 sp each side. Work rnds 85-116 on each of 6 sides.

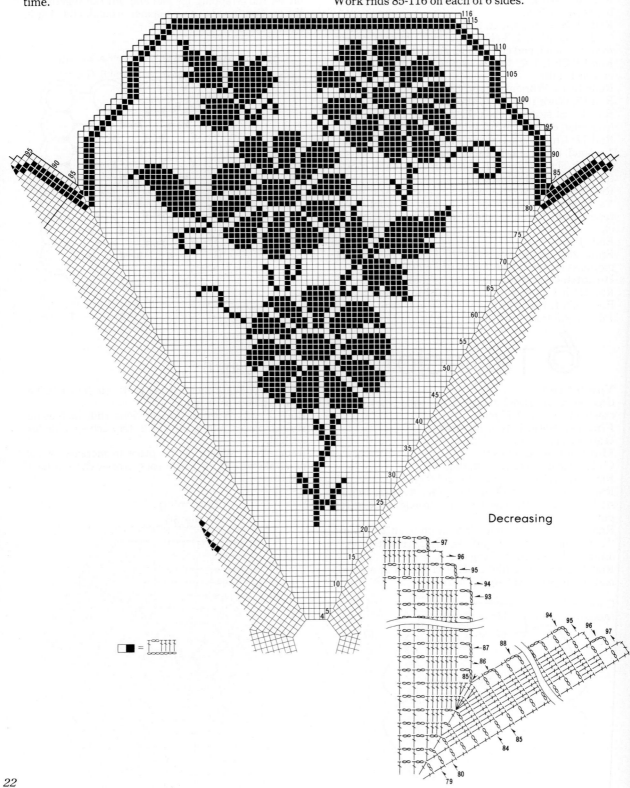

Decreasing

☐ ■ = ⌐ШШ

➤ = join thread in

22

⑨ Tablecloth shown on page 9

You'll Need:
Crochet cotton DMC #3, 103 20-g. balls Orange.
Steel crochet hook size 1.75 mm.
Finished Size: 185 cm in diameter
Gauge: 1 row of dc = 0.9 cm
Making Instructions:
Ch 18, sl st in 1st ch to form ring.
Rnd 1: Ch 3, 35 dc in ring, sl st in 3rd st of beg ch.
Rnd 2: Ch 3, 3-dc puff working 2 dc in 1st dc and 1 dc in next, ch 11, * 4-dc puff in 3 dc, ch 11, repeat from * around, end working ch 5 and tr tr.
Rnd 3: Ch 1, 8 sc in tr tr, * sc in puff st, 15 sc in ch-11 lp, repeat from * around, end 7 sc, sl st in 1st ch.
Rnd 4: Ch 3, dc in sc, ch 2, 2 dc in same st as last dc, * ch 7, work "2 dc, ch 2, 2 dc" in middle st of 15-sc (named shell st), repeat from * around, end sl st in 3rd st of beg ch.
Rnd 5: Shell st in shell st, work "ch 2, 1 dc, ch 2, 1 dc, ch 2" in ch-7.
Rnds 6-10: Work as for previous rnd, increasing sts of ch as shown.
Rnd 11:Work 1 sc and ch 11 alternately around to form 24 lps.

Rnd 12: 13 sc in each lp, sc in each sc around.
Rnd 13: Work 1 sc and ch 11 alternately around.
Rnd 14: Ch 4, 1 dc, sk 2 sts, * 1 dc, ch 1, 1 dc, sk 2 sts, repeat from * around to form 102 patterns, end sl st in 3rd st of beg ch.
Rnds 15-21: Work as for rnd 14 referring to chart.
Rnd 22: Work as for rnd 11, making 34 lps of ch-13.
Rnd 23: 15 sc in lp, sc in sc.
Rnds 24-76: Repeat rnds 4-12.
Rnd 77: 1 sc, ch 7, alternately around.
Rnd 78: Ch 5, dc in sc, (ch 2, 1 dc) 20 times, ch 2, dc in sc, ch 2, dc in same sc as last dc, repeat in same maner around, end sl st in 3rd st of beg ch.
Rnds 79-90: Work dc and ch to form 32 patterns as shown.
Rnd 91: Ch 9, sk 1 sp, 1 hdc, * ch 7, 1 hdc, repeat from around, end sl st in 2nd st of beg ch.

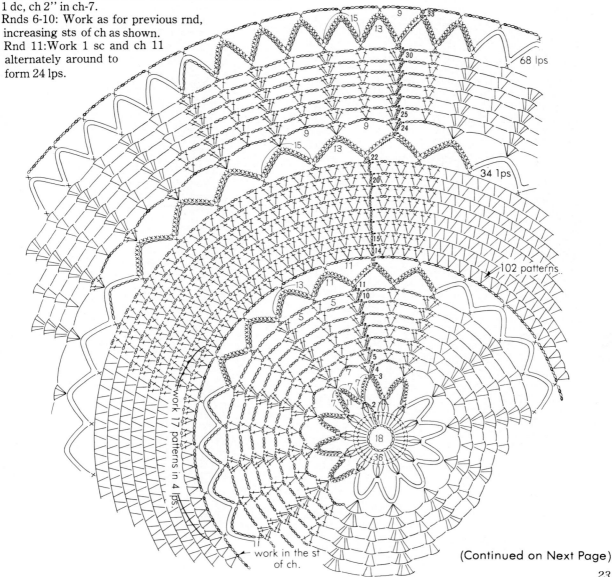

68 lps

34 lps

102 patterns

work 17 patterns in 4 lps.

work in the st of ch.

(Continued on Next Page)

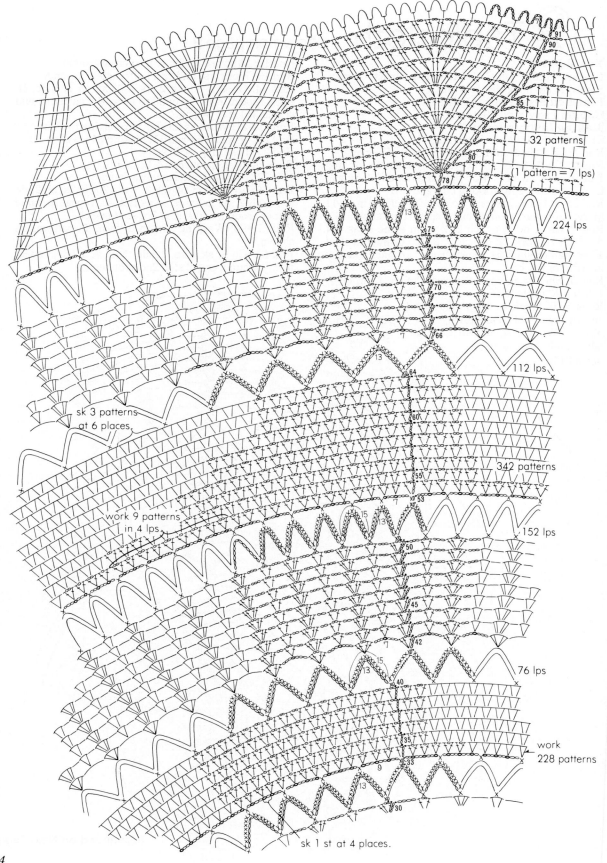

32 patterns

(1 pattern = 7 lps)

224 lps

112 lps

sk 3 patterns
at 6 places.

342 patterns

work 9 patterns
in 4 lps.

152 lps

76 lps

work
228 patterns

sk 1 st at 4 places.

10 Tablecloth

shown on page 10

You'll Need:
Crochet cotton DMC #20 45.5 20-g. balls Beige.
Steel crochet hook size 0.90 mm.
Finished Size: 165 cm by 127.5 cm
Size of Motif: A = 7.5 cm in diameter B = 3 cm in diameter
Gauge: 1 row of dc = 0.5 cm
Making Instructions:
A-motif: Ch 16, sl st in 1st ch to form ring.
Rnd 1: Ch 1, (sc in ch, ch 7) 4 times, end sl st in 1st ch.
Rnd 2: Sl st in ch, ch 3, 4 dc in lp, ch 1, 5 dc in same lp as 4 dc, ch 1, * work "5 dc, ch 1" in next lp, repeat from * around, end sc in 3rd st of beg ch.

Rnd 3: 1 sc, ch 7, alternately around, end ch 3, 4 tr.
Rnd 4: 1 sc, ch 7, alternately around, sl st in 1st sc.
Rnds 5-6: Work as for rnds 2-3.
Rnd 7: Ch 8, 2 dc in same st as ch 8, * work "2 dc, ch 5, 2 dc" in middle st of ch-7, repeat from * around, end sl st in 3rd st of beg ch.
Rnd 8: Work as for rnd 2.
B-motif: Work as for A-motig until 3rd rnd. Work 3rd rnd joining to A-motif with sl st as shown.

Motif A

motif A 374 pieces
motif B 336 pieces

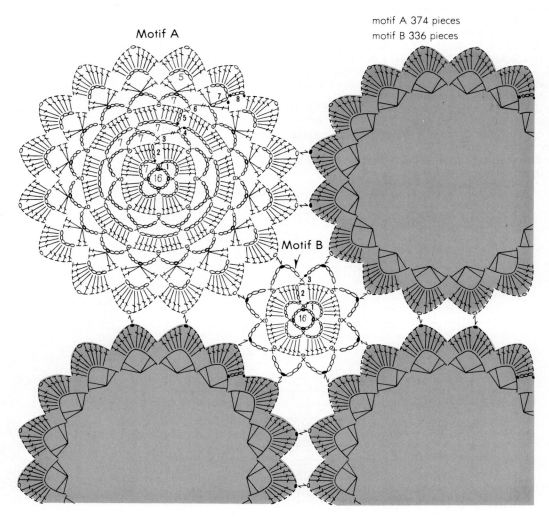

Motif B

= work in ch st previous rnd.

11 Tablecloth

shown on page 11

You'll Need:
Crochet cotton DMC #3, 109 20-g. balls White.
Steel crochet hook size 1.75 mm.

Finished Size: 159 cm by 130 cm

Gauge: 18 squares (1 pattern) = 16.5 cm of pattern
crochet 12 rows = 10 cm

Making Instructions:
Ch 502. Row 1: Ch 5, dc in 9th ch from hook, * ch 2,
sk 2 sts, dc in next st, repeat from * across.

Row 2: Turn the work (each row), make 5 sps as for
previous row. Work 39 dc alternately with 5 sps.

Rows 3-4: Work as for row 2.

Row 5: Referring to chart, work dc and filet crochet.

Row 6: Where at filet crochet, work "ch 1, 5-dc
pop, 1 dc" every other sp.

Rows 7-19: Repeat rows 5-6. Work following repeating 18 rows of 18 squares (1 pattern) as shown on the
chart.

Edging: Work in the manner of braid crochet. Row 1:
Ch 5, work "1 dc, ch 1, 1 dc" in 1st st, ch 2, secure to
pattern crochet with sc. Turn, "2 dc, ch 1, 1 dc" in
ch-1, turn, ch 4, "2 dc, ch 1, 1 dc" in ch-1, ch 2, sc in
pattern crochet, turn, "2 dc, ch 1, 1 dc" in ch-1, turn
ch 3, 1 dc, ch 1, 1 dc, continue in same way around
the pattern crochet working corners as shown. End
sl st in 1st ch instead of making last ch st.

Row 2: Ch 1, 1 sc, ch 2, 1 sc, work "(2-dc puff, ch 4)
3 times, 2-dc puff" in ch-4 lp, "1 sc, ch 2, 1 sc" in
ch-3 lp, continue in same manner around, making
5 2-dc puff in corner lp.

Row 3: 5 sc in each ch-4. Work 1 sl st, ch 2, 1 sl st,
over the lp between 4-puff sts.

Chart on Measurements

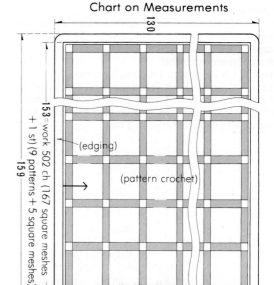

153 = work 502 ch (167 square meshes) + 1 st) (9 patterns + 5 square meshes)

159

3 = 3 rows

124 = 149 rows
(8 patterns + 5 rows)

(edging)

(pattern crochet)

130

Sts of pattern Crochet

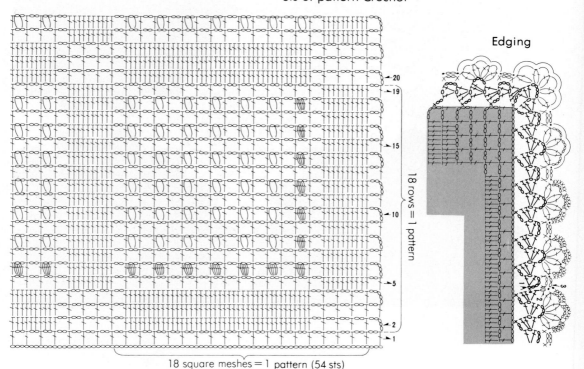

18 square meshes = 1 pattern (54 sts)

18 rows = 1 pattern

Edging

26

12 Tablecloth

shown on pages 12 - 13

You'll Need:
Crochet cotton DMC #20 23 20-g. balls White. Steel crochet hook sizze 0.90 mm.
Finished Size: 120 cm square
Size of Motif: A=15 cm in diameter B=6 cm in diameter
Gauge: 1 row of dc=0.5 cm
Making Instructions:
A-motif: Ch 8, sl st in 1st ch to form ring.
Rnd 1: Ch3, 23 dc in ring, sl st in 3rd st of beg ch.
Rnd 2: Ch 6, * sk 1 dc, dc in dc, ch 3, repeat from * around, end sl st in 3rd st of beg ch.
Rnd 3: Sl st in ch, ch 7, dc in lp, work "1 dc, ch 4, 1 dc" in each lp around, end sl st in 3rd st of beg ch.

Rnd 4: Work as for previous rnd, making "2 dc, ch 5, 2 dc" in each lp around.
Rnd 5: Work 11 dc in each lp around.
Rnd 6: Sl st in each st of 4 dc, ch 1, sc in dc, * ch 9, sc in middle dc, repeat from * around, end sl st in 1st ch.
Rnds 7-10: Work as for rnds 3-6.
Rnds 11-13: Work filet crochet making 1 dc, ch 1, alternately.
Rnd 14: Work net st (1 sc, ch 5) around, end working ch 2, 1 dc, instead of ch 5.
Rnd 15: Sc in lp, ch 3, 3-ch p, ch 3, continue in same way around, sl st in 1st sc. End off.
B-motif: Work as for A-motif until rnd 5. Work rnd 5 joining to A-motifs with sl st as shown.

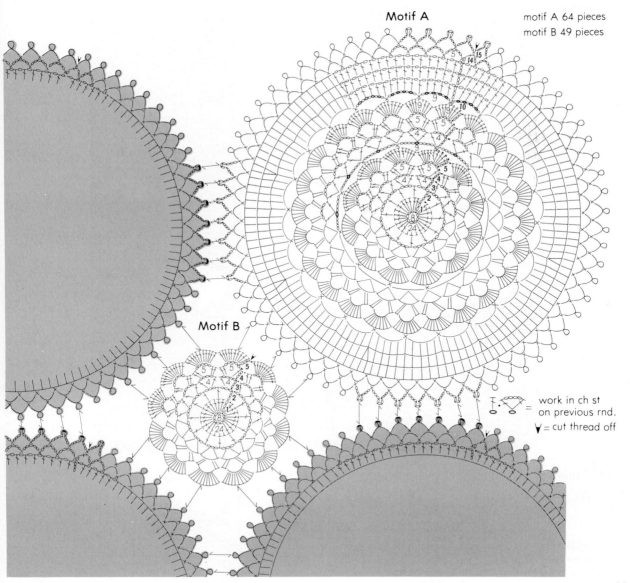

Motif A

motif A 64 pieces
motif B 49 pieces

Motif B

$\underset{\circ\ \circ}{\top}\underset{\circ}{\curvearrowright}$ = work in ch st on previous rnd.
Ⅴ = cut thread off

13 Tablecloth

shown on page 14

You'll Need:
Crochet cotton DMC #5, 62 20-g. balls Beige. Steel crochet hook size 1.25 mm.
Finished Size: 150 cm square
Size of Motif: 12.5 cm square
Gauge: 1 row of dc = 0.7 cm
Making Instructions:
Ch 8, sl st in 1st ch to form ring.
Row 1: Ch 5, (dc in ring, ch 2) 7 times, sl st in 3rd st of beg ch.
Row 2: Ch 1, * 3 sc in lp, ch 1, repeat from * around, end 3 sc, sc in 1st ch.
Row 3: Ch 5, tr in last sc, * ch 5, dc in ch, ch 5, tr in ch, ch 1, tr in same st as tr, repeat from * around, end sl st in 4th st of beg ch.
Row 4: Work corners in same way as for previous row, making 5 patterns each side as shown on the chart below.

Row 5: Work as for previous row.
Row 6: Work corners as for previous row, making 4 dc each in ch-3 lp.
Row 7: Make 2 arcs of ch-5 net st on the corner, make 3 arcs of ch-9 net st on the side between corners.
Row 9: Work "3 sc, 3-ch p, 3 sc" in ch-5 lp, "4 sc, 3-ch p, 3 sc, 3-ch p, 4 sc" in ch-9 lp. Having worked the net st of ch-9 up to the middle of 3rd arc, turn the work, make 2 arcs of ch-9, turn back to the middle of 2nd arc working sc and p as shown, make 1 arc in same way. End working sc and p over the remaining lps. Work finishing 1 side each in same way.
From 2nd motif, work p joining to previous motif as shown. Make 12 rows of 12 motifs.

Sts of Motifs & Joining

motif 144 pieces

Pattern St

① insert hook as arrow, draw thread through.

② work in next st and the st after in same way as for ①.

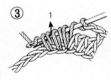
③

④

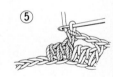
⑤

14 Tablecloth

shown on page 15

You'll Need:
Crochet cotton DMC #15, 31.5. 20-g. balls White.
Steel crochet hook size 1.00 mm. White linen 92 cm
square.

Gauge: Filet crochet: 17 squares = 10 cm 18.5 rows =
10 cm

Finished Size: 71 cm by 65 cm (each piece)

Making Instructions:
Ch 310. Row 1: Ch 5, dc in 8th st from hook, *ch 2,
sk 2 ch, 1 dc, repeat from * across. Make 103 squares.
Row 2: Turn the work, ch 8 to from 1 square. Work
filet crochet of 1 dc, ch 2, across, making 3 dc for
each bl.
Row 3: Turn, ch 5. Work filet crochet making patterns
as shown, end ch 2, dtr, to form 1 sp.
Rows 4-8: Work straight as for rows 2-3, increasing
one side as shown.
Rows 9-10: Work straight.
Rows 11-16: Work decreasing 1 sp each row increased
side. Decrease working ch 5 at the beginning, dc
and dtr at a time at the end.
Rows 17-129: Work filet crochet as for fows 1-16,
making patterns as shown on the chart.
Edging: Work on 3 sides. On even side, work sc,
3-ch p. On decreased side, work "3 dc, ch 2, 3 dc"
1 sc. On increased side, work 3 dc, 1 sc.

Make 4 pieces in same manner.
Cut fabric round 92 cm in diameter, turn raw edge
1 cm to wrong side, sew on top edge of the worked
lace.
Spread on the table of 90 cm in diameter.

Chart on Measurements

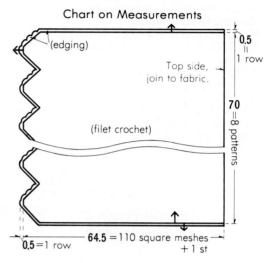

Joining

Bottom Side & Edging

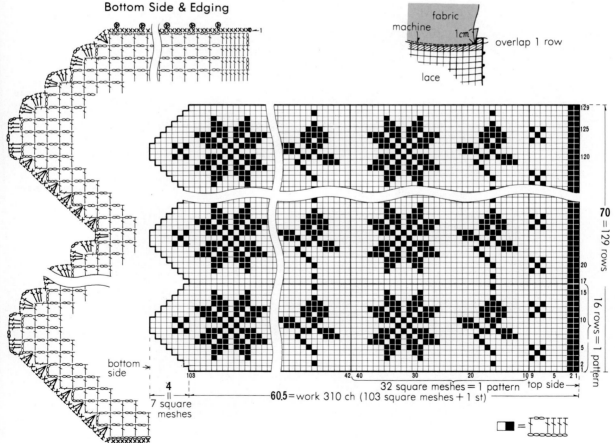

29

5 Tablecloth shown on page 5

You'll Need:
Crochet cotton DMC #20, 40 20-g. balls White. Steel crochet hook size 1.00 mm.
Finished Size: 142 cm in diameter
Gauge: 1 row of dc = 0.7 cm
Size of Motif: 5.5 cm in diameter
Making Instructions:
Motif: Ch 8, sl st in 1st ch to form ring.
Rnd 1: Ch 5, (1 dc, ch 2) 11 times in ring, sl st in 3rd st of beg ch.
Rnd 2: Ch 1, 1 sc, work "1 sc, ch 4, 1 sc" in lp, sc in dc. Continue in same manner around, end sl st in 1st ch.
Rnd 3: Sl st in sts to proceed to the middle of lp, * 1 sc, ch 5, repeat from * around.
Rnd 4: Ch 1, work "1 sc, 1 hdc, 5 dc, 1 hdc, 1 sc" in each lp around, end sl st in 1st ch.

Edging of center motif: Rnd 5: Sl st continued from rnd 4 to proceed to the middle of petal, * 1 sc, ch 6, repeat from * around, end sl st in 1st sc.
Rnd 6: Ch 1, 10 dc in each lp around, sl st in 1st ch.
Rnd 7: Ch 5, work "1 dc, ch 2" every 2 sc around, end sl st in 3rd st of beg ch.
Rnd 8: Ch 1, work "2 sc, ch 3, 2 sc" in each lp around, end sl st in 1st ch. End off.
2nd-rnd-motif: Make 8 pieces of center motif joining with sl st where indicated.
Pattern crochet A: Rnd 1: Join cotton in motif, ch 6, tr tr in next motif, * ch 7, dc in the middle of next petal, ch 5, (sc in petal, ch 5) 2 times, dc in next petal, ch 7, 2 tr tr at a time, repeat from * around, end sl st in 1st tr tr.
Rnd 2: Ch 1, * sc in 2 sts at at time, 9 sc in ch-7, (7 sc in ch-5) 3 times, 9 sc in ch-7, repeat from * around, sl st in 1st ch.

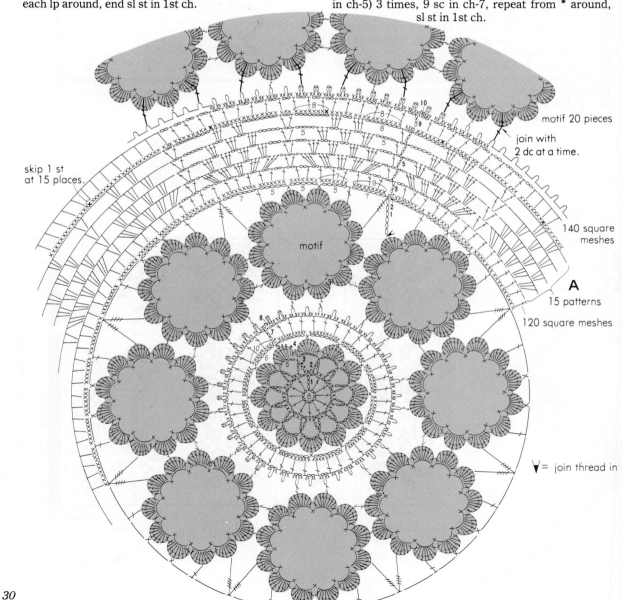

skip 1 st at 15 places.

motif 20 pieces

join with 2 dc at a time.

140 square meshes

A

15 patterns

120 square meshes

motif

= join thread in

Rnd 3: Ch 5, * sk 2 sc (ro 1 sc), dc in sc, ch 2, repeat from * around to form 120 sps, end sl st in 3rd st of beg ch.
Rnds 4-7: Work dc and ch making each pattern in 8 sps previous rnd as shown.
Rnd 8: Sc in each st around.
Rnd 9: Work as for rnd 3, making 140 sps.
Rnd 10: Work "2 sc, ch 3, 2 sc" in each lp around. End off.

3rd-rnd-motif: Make 20 pieces of center motif joininig with sl st where indicated.
Work pattern crochet B - F as for A, joining motifs in position.
Pattern crochet G: Rnds 1-3: Work as for A.
Rnds 4-8: Work making each pattern in 9 sps each around.
Rnd 9: Work "(1 dc, 3-ch p) 5 times, 1 dc" in ch-3 lp, "ch 4, 1 sc, ch 4" in the middle of ch-9 lp.

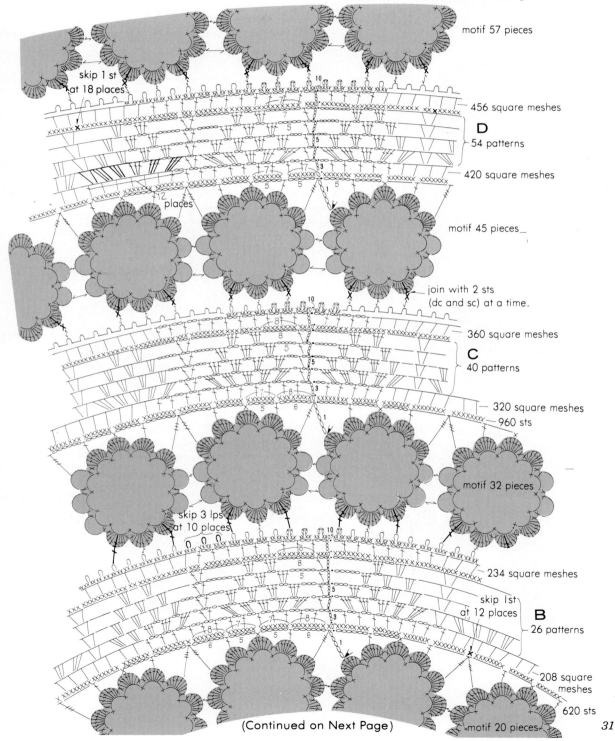

motif 57 pieces

skip 1 st at 18 places

456 square meshes

D
54 patterns

420 square meshes

12 places

motif 45 pieces

join with 2 sts (dc and sc) at a time.

360 square meshes

C
40 patterns

320 square meshes
960 sts

motif 32 pieces

skip 3 lps at 10 places

234 square meshes

skip 1st at 12 places

B
26 patterns

208 square meshes

620 sts

motif 20 pieces

(Continued on Next Page)

31

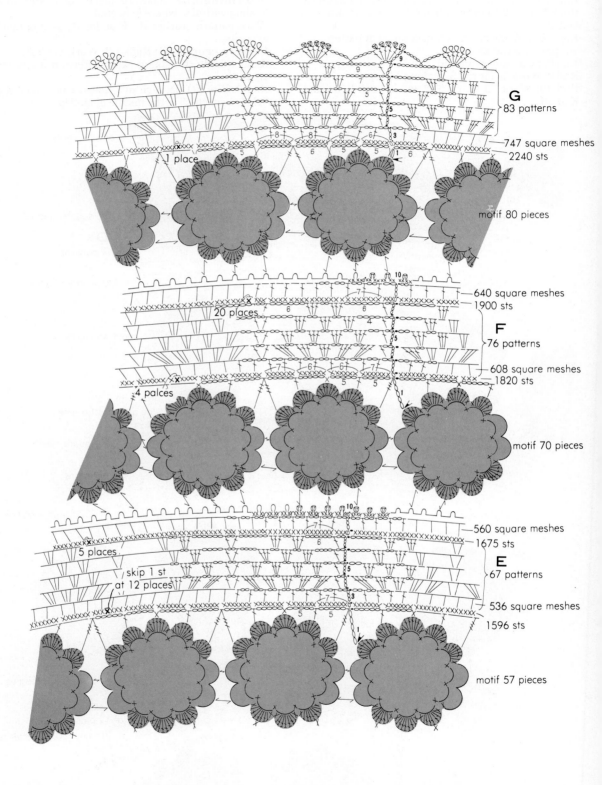

G
83 patterns

747 square meshes
2240 sts

1 place

motif 80 pieces

640 square meshes
1900 sts

20 places

F
76 patterns

608 square meshes
1820 sts

4 palces

motif 70 pieces

560 square meshes
1675 sts

5 places

E
67 patterns

skip 1 st
at 12 places

536 square meshes
1596 sts

motif 57 pieces

CURTAINS

Instructions on page 49

Instructions on page 50

Instructions on page 54

Instructions on page 58

BEDSPREADS

22

Instructions on page 63

23

Instructions on page 110

Instructions on page 120

25

Instructions on page 117

16 Curtain shown on page 33

You'll Need:
Crochet cotton DMC #5, 127.5 20-g. balls White.
Steel crochet hook size 1.25mm.
Finished Size: 194 cm wide by 203.5cm long.
Size of Motif: Octagon of 4 cm each side
Gauge: 1 row of dc = 0.6cm
Making Instructions:
Motif: Make a loop at the end of cotton.
Rnd 1: Ch 3, 2 dc in 1p, (ch 3, 3 dc in 1p) 3 times, ch 3, sl st in 3rd st of beg ch.
Rnd 2: Ch 3, dc in same st as ch 3, dc in dc, 2 dc in next dc, ch 5, continue in same way around, sl st in 3rd st of beg ch.
Rnds 3-8: Work 2 dc in edge dc, increasing sts of ch as shown.
From 2nd motif, work dc on 8th rnd joining to previous motif.
Make 21 rows of 20 motifs.
Edging: Rnd 1: Join cotton in edge dc of the motif indicated, ch 1, sc in 17 dc, ch 25, 17 sc, ch 22, sc in between motifs, ch 11, tr in ch st of previous motif, ch 10, 17 sc. Continue in same manner around.
Rnds 2-4: DC in each st around, working corners as shown.

Chart on Measuremetns   motif 420 pieces

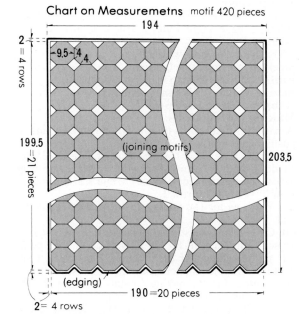

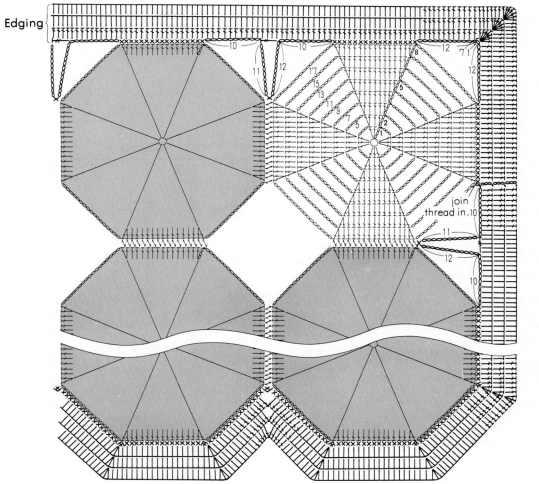

As for the way of joining motifs, see page 130.

17 Curtain shown on page 34

You'll Need:
Crochet cotton DMC #20, 20-g. ball; 62.5 balls White, 3 balls Light Pink, 2.5 balls Brown, 2 balls each of Deep Pink, Orange, Green, Dark Green, 1.5 balls each of Yellow, Blue.
Steel crochet hook size 0.90 mm.
Finished Size: 202 cm wide by 172 cm long
Size of Motif: A = 25 cm in diameter
Gauge: 1 row of dc = 0.6 cm
Making Instructions:
A-motif: Make motifs (1)-(6) with indicated colors in position previously.
(1): Ch 20. Row 1: Ch 1, sc in last st of base ch, 2 hdc, 14 dc, 2 hdc, 3 sc in 1st st, continue in same way across the counter side of base ch, end sl st in 1st ch.
Row 2: Work as for row 1.
(2): Work as for (1), joining to 1st row of (1) at the end.
(3): Ch 10, sl st in 1st ch to form ring. Row 1: Ch 1, 15 sc in ring, sl st in 1st ch. Row 2: Ch 1, 1 sc, ch 5, 4-tr puff working 2-tr each in next 2 sc, ch 5, 1 sc, continue in same manner around, sl st in 1st sc.
(4): Work as for (3), making 4 petals as shown. Work 3-ch p at the end of 4th petal to join to (1).
(5): Ch 10, sl st in 1st ch to form ring. Row 1: Ch 3, 17 dc in ring, sl st in 3rd st of beg ch. Row 2: Ch 1, 1 sc, ch 4, sk 2 dc, 1 sc, continue in same way around, sl st in 1st ch. Row 3: Ch 1, work "1 sc, 1 hdc, 3 dc, 1 hdc, 1 sc" in each 1p around, sl st in 1st ch. Row 4: Work 1 sc, ch 6, alternately around. Make each sc in the sc 2nd row, turning 3rd row toward you. Row 5: Work as for row 3, making 4-ch p where indicated on the chart to join to (2) and (3).
(6): Ch 10, sl in 1st ch to form ring.
Row 1: Ch 1, 15 sc in ring. Row 2: Ch 4, 3-tr pop in sc, * ch 3, 4-tr pop in next sc, repeat from * around, end sl st in 4th st of beg ch. Row 3: Work net st (1 sc, ch 6) around.
Row 4: Sl st in 3 sts, * sc in the middle of lp, ch 20, sl st in 3rd st from the top of ch-20, ch 3, repeat from * around.
Row 5: Ch 1, * sc in ch-3, 28 dc in ch-17 lp, sc in ch-3, repeat from * around, making þ to join to (4), (2), (5), and (3) as shown on the chart.
Lace surrounding (1)-(6): Work with White.
Rnd 1: Join cotton in (6) where indicated, ch 1, (1 sc, ch 7, Y-st, ch 7) 2 times, 1 sc, ch 7, ch 5, 2-tr puff in 5th st from hook, (ch 4, tr in puff st, ch 4, hdc in puff st) 3 times, ch 4, 3 sts (2 tr in puff st and q tr in 1st st of beg ch) at a time, ch 7. Continue in same way around, working 4 sts (2 tr each) at a time between (2) and (5), (5) and (3).
Rnd 2: Work "1 sc, 2 hdc, 6 dc, 2 hdc, 1 sc" in each lp around.
Rnd 3: Sl st in 3 sts, work net st (1 sc, ch 5) around.
Rnd 4: Sl st in 2 sts, ch 3, dc in lp, ch 3, 2-dc puff in same lp as dc, ch 2, sc in next lp, * ch 2, 2-dc puff in lp, ch 3, 2-dc puff in same lp, ch 2, sc in next lp, repeat from * around.
Rnds 5-16: Work as for rnds 3-4.

Rnd 17: Work net st of ch-8.
Rnd 18: Work as for rnd 2, making 5-ch p and 7-ch p as shown.
B-motif: Ch 10, sl st in 1st ch to form ring.
Rnd 1: Ch 5, (dc in ring, ch 2) 11 times, sl st in 3rd st of beg ch.
Rnd 2: Work 4-dc pop, ch 4, alternately around, end working ch 2, 1 hdc, instead of ch 4.
Rnd 3: Work net st of ch-6 around, end 3, 1 dc.
Rnd 4: * 1 sc, 9 dc in lp, sc in enxt lp, ch 6, repeat from * around, end ch 3, 1 dc.
Rnd 5: Work dc in each dc alternately with ch 1, "2 dc, ch 3, 2 dc" in each lp.
Rnd 6: Where at ch 1, work net st of 1 sc, ch-5. Where at ch-3 lp, work ch 2, (2 dc, ch 3) 2 times, 2 dc, ch 2. From next rnd, work 1 pattern each.
Rnd 7: Ch 3, 1 dc, ch 2, sc in lp, (ch 5, sc in next lp) 6 times, ch 2, 2 dc.
Rnds 8-13: Work as for rnd 7, turning the work each rnd.
Rnd 14: Ch 3, 3 dc. End off. Work remaining sides in same manner.

Coloring

motifs	colors	sizes
(1)	dark green	3.5 cm × 1.8 cm
(2)	green	
(3)	blue	2 cm in diameter
(4)	orange	2.5 cm × 1.8 cm
(5)	1 row white / 2-3 rows orange / 4-5 rows yellow	3 cm in diameter
(6)	1-2 rows deep pink / 3-5 rows pale pink	7.5 cm in diameter

1 = 2 rows

join to A-motif

D

200 = 8 pieces

A
25

C

B

11

1 = 2 rows

(joining motifs)

A-48 pieces
B-35 pieces
C-24 pieces
D-4 pieces
E-7 pieces

150 = 6 pieces

172

D

1 = 2 pieces

(bottom border) (edging)

E

20

202

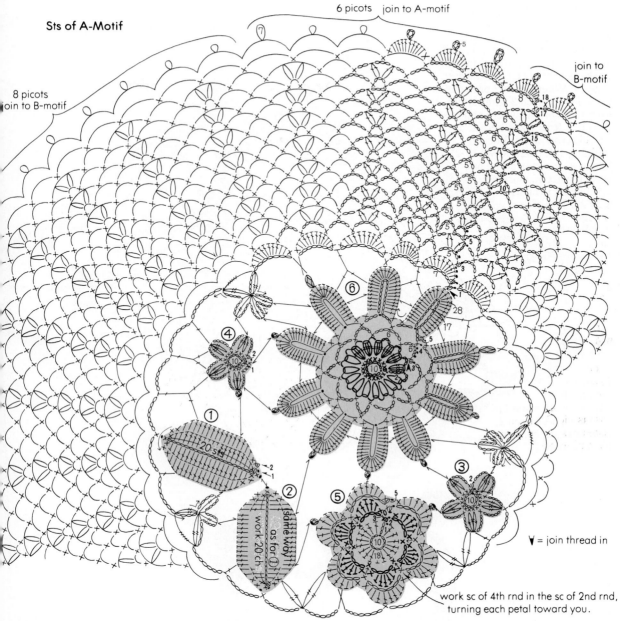

Sts of A-Motif

6 picots   join to A-motif

join to B-motif

8 picots
join to B-motif

28

17

⑥

④

10

2
1

① 20 sts

10   2
1

② same way work 20ch
as for ①

⑤

10

18

③

10

V = join thread in

work sc of 4th rnd in the sc of 2nd rnd,
turning each petal toward you.

Trimming of B-motif: Row 1: Work net st following the sts of ch indicated.
Row 2: Work "5 dc, 5-ch p (on the 3rd st of p, work sl st to join to A), 5 dc" in lp, sc in next lp. Continue in same way around, making 7-ch p on the top of each motif.
C-motif: Make half of B-motif.
D-motif: Make quarter of B-motif.
Edging: Work along the edge of curtain.
Row 1: Work filet crochet (1 dc, ch 3) around, making Y-st where at A-motif as shown.
Row 2: Dc in each st around.
Bottom border: Make E-motif with Brown previously. Ch 6, sl st in 1st ch to form ring. Row 1: Ch 10, (dc in ring, ch 7) 3 times, sl st in 3rd st of beg ch.
Row 2: Work "1 sc, 1 hdc, 3 dc, 5-ch p, 3 dc, 1 hdc, 1 sc, ch 13" in each lp around.

From 2nd piece, work joining with sl st where at the middle of lp and p. Join 74 motifs crossway.
Row 1: Work along the bottom edge. Join cotton in, 1 sc, ch 3, * 1 sc, ch 4, repeat from * across, ending with 1 sc, ch 3, 1 sc.
Rows 2-6: Turn each row. Ch 7, upside-down of Y-st, * ch 4, upside-down of Y-st, repeat from * across, end ch 3, 1 tr.
Row 7: Join to E-motif working 5-ch p at the middle of dc.
Join cotton in left end of the joined-motif, work turning each row. Row 1: Work 1 sc, ch 9, alternately across.
Row 2: Work "1 sc, 2 hdc, 7 dc, 2 hdc, 1 sc" in each lp across.
Row 3: Ch 5, 1 dc, * ch 4, 1 sc, ch 4, 1 dc, repeat from * across, end ch 1, 1 tr.

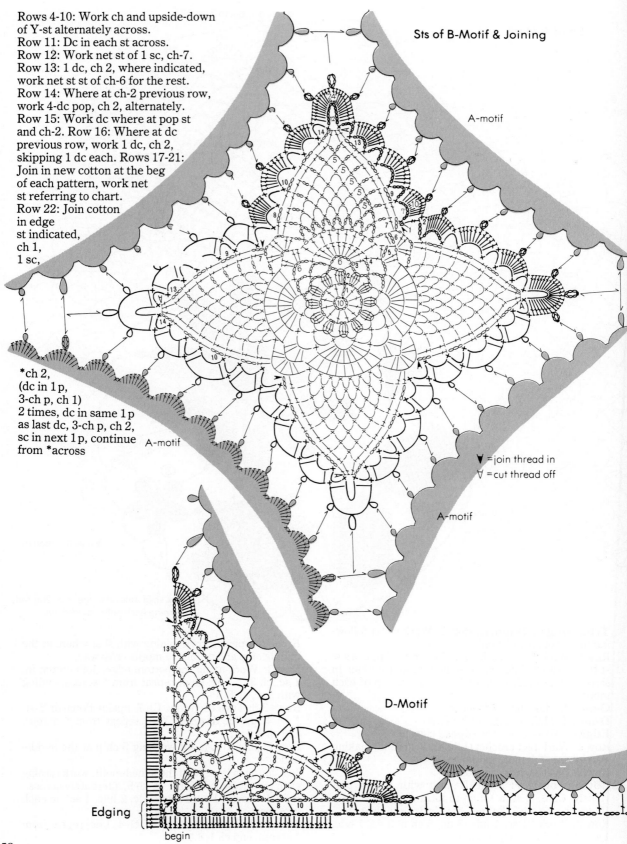

Rows 4-10: Work ch and upside-down
of Y-st alternately across.
Row 11: Dc in each st across.
Row 12: Work net st of 1 sc, ch-7.
Row 13: 1 dc, ch 2, where indicated,
work net st st of ch-6 for the rest.
Row 14: Where at ch-2 previous row,
work 4-dc pop, ch 2, alternately.
Row 15: Work dc where at pop st
and ch-2. Row 16: Where at dc
previous row, work 1 dc, ch 2,
skipping 1 dc each. Rows 17-21:
Join in new cotton at the beg
of each pattern, work net
st referring to chart.
Row 22: Join cotton
in edge
st indicated,
ch 1,
1 sc,

*ch 2,
(dc in 1 p,
3-ch p, ch 1)
2 times, dc in same 1 p
as last dc, 3-ch p, ch 2,
sc in next 1 p, continue
from *across

Sts of B-Motif & Joining

A-motif

A-motif

A-motif

▼ = join thread in
▽ = cut thread off

D-Motif

Edging {

begin

52

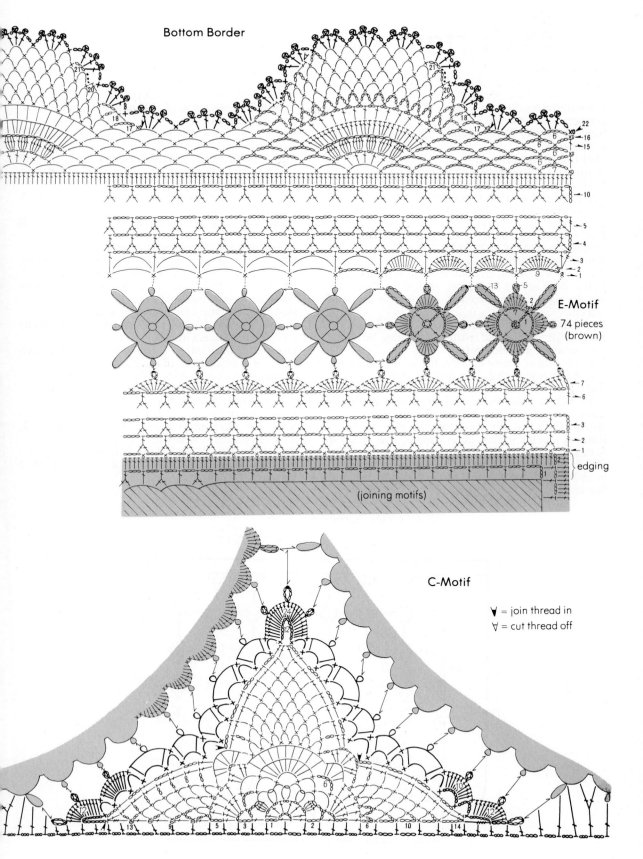

Bottom Border

E-Motif
74 pieces
(brown)

edging
(joining motifs)

C-Motif

∀ = join thread in
∀ = cut thread off

18 Curtain shown on page 36

You'll Need:
Crochet cotton DMC #20, 71 20-g. balls White. Steel crochet hook size 0.90 mm.
Finished Size: 197 cm wide by 175 cm long
Gauge: 1 row of dc = 0.5 cm
Size of Motif: A, B = 12 cm in diameter C = 4.5 cm in diameter
Making Instructions:
A-motif: Ch 8, sl st in 1st ch to form ring.
Rnd 1: Ch 1, 16 sc in ring, sl st in 1st ch.
Rnd 2: Work 1 sc, ch 3, every other sc.
Rnd 3: Work "1 sc, 1 hdc, 3 dc, 1 hdc, 1 sc" in each lp around.
Rnd 4: Make the lp of "1 sc, ch 5", working sc in wrong side of the sc on 2nd rnd.
Rnd 5: Work sts in lp as for rnd 3.
Rnd 6: Sl st in 4 sts, ch 5, dc in same st as last sl st, * ch 5, dc in middle st of petal, ch 2, dc in same st as last dc, repeat from * around, end sl st in 3rd st of beg ch.
Rnd 7: 4 dc in ch-2, "ch 3, 1 dc, ch 3" in ch-5.
Rnds 8-12: Make leaf pattern, working in same manner as for previous rnd.
Rnd 13: 4 dc at a time on 6-dc, net st of ch-5 for the rest. End working ch 2, 1 dc, instead of ch 5.
Rnd 14: 1 sc, * ch 3, work "1 dc, 3-ch p, 1 dc, 5-ch p, 1 dc, 3-ch p, 1 dc" in lp, ch 3, sc in next lp, repeat from * around, end sl st in 1st sc. End off.
B-motif: Ch 6, sl st in 1st ch to form ring.
Rnd 1: Ch 5, (dc in ring, ch 2) 7 times, sl st in 3rd st of beg ch.
Rnd 2: Sl st in ch, ch 3, 1 dc, ch 3, * sc in dc, ch 3, 2 dc in ch-2, ch 3, repeat from * around, sl st in 3rd st of beg ch.

Rnd 3: Ch 1, * sc in the middle of 2-dc, ch 7, repeat from * around, end sl st in 1st ch.
Rnd 4: Work as for rnd 5 of A-motif.
Rnds 5-7: Work net st of ch-7 around. End each rnd working ch 3, 1 tr.
Rnd 8: 1 sc, ch 5, 6-tr puff, ch 5, continue in same manner around.
Rnds 9-11: Work net st of ch-7, increasing the number of lps around. Work rnd 9 making dc in sc between lps previous rnd.
Rnd 12: Work as for rnd 14 of A-motif, joining to A as shown.
Make 13 rows of 14 motifs, joining A and B alternately.
C-motif: Ch 8, sl st in 1st ch to form ring.
Rnd 1: Ch 3, (dc in ring, 3-ch p, 2 dc in ring) 7 times, dc in ring, 3-ch p, dc in ring, sl st in 3rd st of beg ch.
Rnd 2: Ch 8, * sk 2 sts, dc in dc, ch 5, repeat from * around, sl st in 3rd st of beg ch.
Rnd 3: Work net st of ch-5 around, end ch 2, 1 dc.
Rnd 4: Work as for rnd 14 of A-motif. Work middle p joining to adjacent motifs.
D-motif: Make half of C-motif. Work turning each rnd, join to adjacent motifs on rnd 4.
Edging: Work on 3 sides of the joined-motif.
Row 1: Stitch along making edges even as shown.
Row 2: Work net st of ch-5.
Row 3: Work "1 sc, ch 2, 3 dc" in each lp.
Rows 4-8: Work net st of ch-6. When to work row 7, inc sts at the curve where indicated.
Row 9: Work "4 dc, ch 3, 4 dc" in lp, sc in next lp.
Row 10: Work "2 dc, ch 3, 2 dc" in ch-3, ch 7 between.

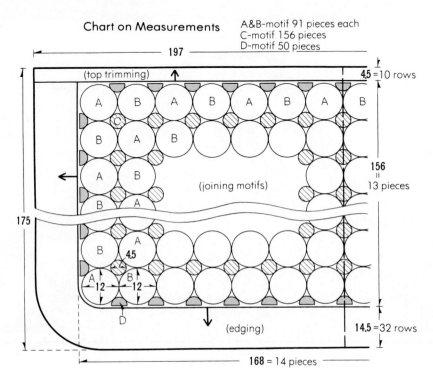

Chart on Measurements

A&B-motif 91 pieces each
C-motif 156 pieces
D-motif 50 pieces

197

(top trimming)

4.5 = 10 rows

A B A B A B A B

B A B

A B

(joining motifs)

156
=
13 pieces

175

B A

B 4.5

A B
-12- -12-

D

(edging)

14.5 = 32 rows

168 = 14 pieces

A-Motif

C-Motif

D-Motif

B-Motif

D

C

D

A

B

A

B

as for the sc on 4th
rnd of A-motif, work
in wrong side of the
sc on 2nd rnd.

Sts on the Corner

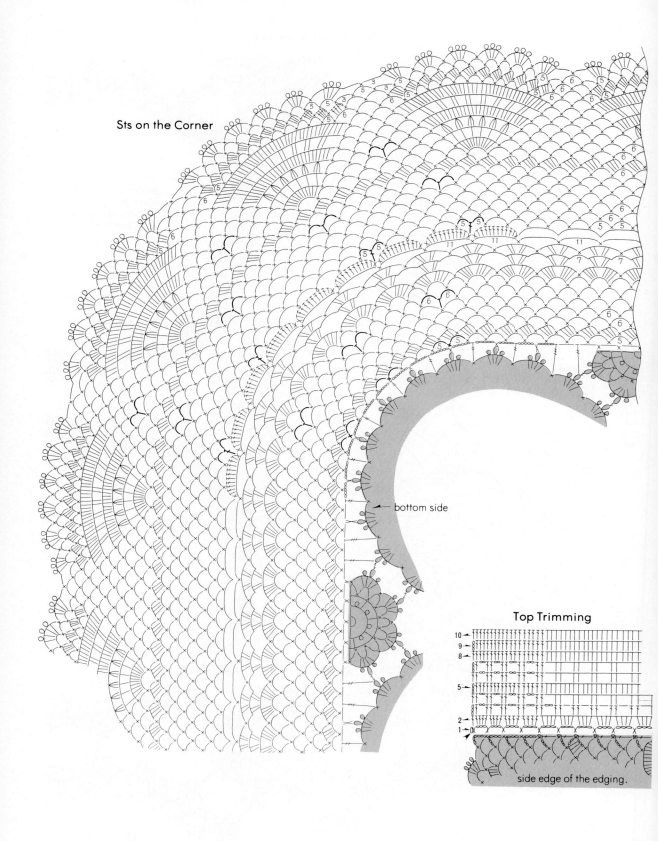

bottom side

Top Trimming

side edge of the edging.

Edging

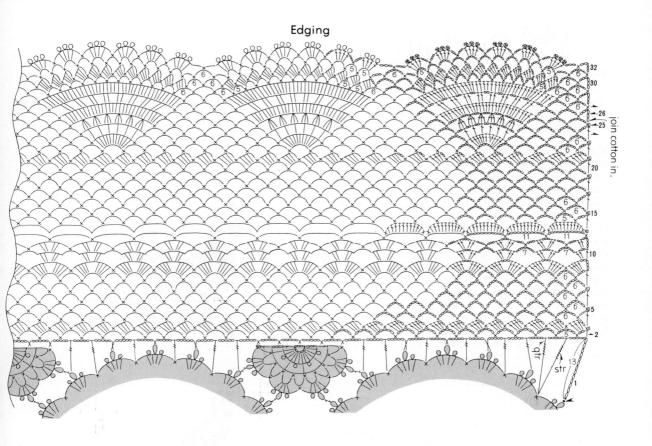

Row 11: Work as for previous row, making ch 3, 1 sc, ch 3, between.
Row 12: Work ch 11, 1 sc, alternately.
Row 13: Work "1 sc, 1 hdc, 8 dc, 1 hdc, 1 sc" in each lp.
Rows 14-20: Net st, increasing at the curve on 14th and 19th row where indicated.
Row 21: Work as for row 3.
Row 22: Net st of ch-6.
Row 23: 11 dc in the lp indicated on the chart.
Row 24: Alternate 1 dc, ch 2, at 11-dc previous row.
Row 25: Ch 3, 3 dc at a time, at the repetition of ch 2, 1 dc previous row.

Row 26: Dc in each st at the pattern.
Row 27: Work ch 2, 2 dc, at the pattern.
Row 28: Dc in each st at the pattern.
Rows 29-31: Work as for rows 2-4.
Row 32: Work as for 14th rnd of A-motif.
Top trimming: Work along top edge.
Row 1: Work as for edging, making edge line even.
Row 2: Work dc along. Rows 3-4: Alternate 2 dc, ch 2. Rows 5-7: Work as for rows 2-4. Rows 8-10: Work dc along.

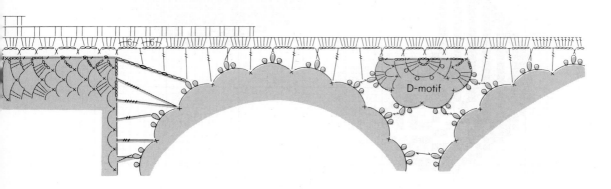

D-motif

19 Curtain shown on page 38

You'll Need:
Crochet cotton DMC #20, 21 20-g. balls White. Steel crochet hook size 0.90 mm.
Finished Size: 82.5 cm wide by 177 cm long
Gauge: Filet crochet: 20.5 squares = 10 cm
20.5 rows = 10 cm

Making Instructions:
Make bottom border first. Ch 165. Row 1: Ch 3, 3 dc (ch 6, sk 5 sts, 5 sc, ch 6, sk 5 sts, 4 dc) 3 times, (ch 2, 1 dc) 2 times, 1 dc, ch 3, sk 2 sts, 1 sc, ch 3, sk 2 sts, 4 dc, (ch 3, sk 2 sts, 1 sc, ch 3, sk 2 sts, 2 dc) 3 times, (ch 2, 1 dc) 7 times, 3 dc, (ch 2, 1 dc) 11 times, 1 dc, ch 3, sk 2 sts, 1 sc, ch 3, sk 2 sts, 4 dc.
Rows 2-13: Work as for 1st row, making patterns as shown. Turn each row, increasing bottom side.
Rows 14-25: Work pattern in same manner. Dec bottom side working sl st as shown.
Rows 26-169: Repeat rows 2-25.
Filet crochet: Pick up sts along the top of bottom border.
Row 1: Ch 3, 6 dc, ch 3, sk 2 sts, 1 sc, ch 3, sk 2 sts, 7 dc, (ch 2, sk 2 sts, 1 dc) 57 times, 6 dc, ch 3, sk 2 sts, 1 sc, ch 3, sk 2 sts, 7 dc.

Row 2: Work as for 1st row, making ch 5 at the pattern each side.
Rows 3-290: Work in same manner as for 1st and 2nd row.
Work "ch 2, 1 dc" for each sp, "3 dc" for each bl.
Finish top edge working 4 rows of dc along.

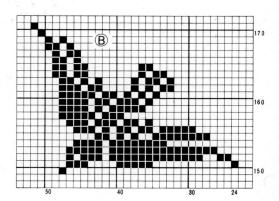

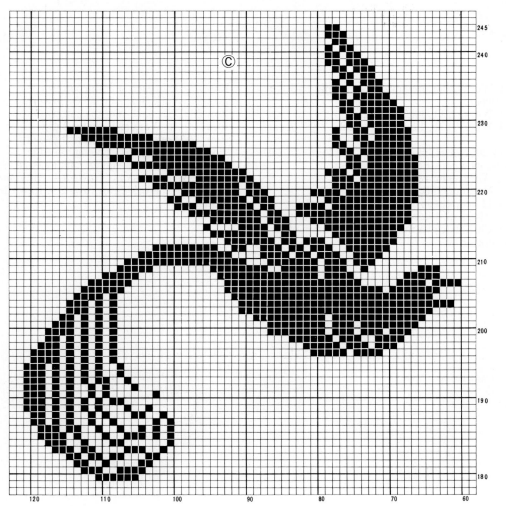

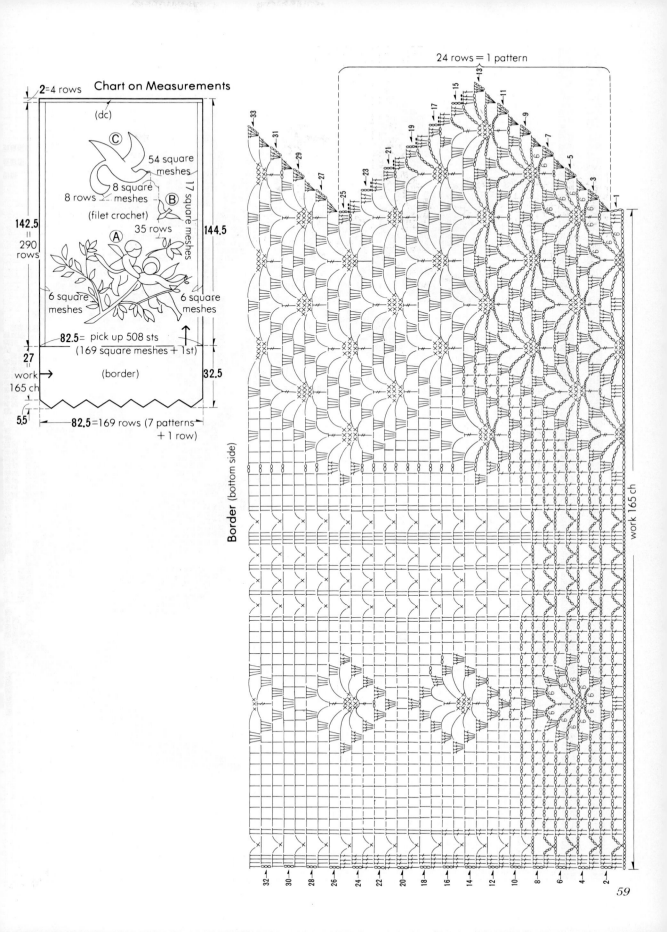

Chart on Measurements

2=4 rows

(dc)

54 square meshes

8 square meshes

8 rows

(filet crochet)

35 rows

17 square meshes

142.5 = 290 rows

144.5

6 square meshes

6 square meshes

82.5 = pick up 508 sts (169 square meshes + 1st)

27

work 165 ch

(border)

32.5

5.5

82.5 = 169 rows (7 patterns + 1 row)

24 rows = 1 pattern

Border (bottom side)

work 165 ch

59

20 Bedspread

shown on page 39

You'll Need:
Crochet cotton DMC #3, 254.5 20-g. balls Gold Brown. Steel crochet hook size 1.60 mm.
Finished Size: 192 cm by 288 cm
Size of Motif: 24 cm square
Gauge: 1 row of dc = 0.8 cm
Making Instructions:
Motif: Ch 12, sl st in 1st ch to form ring.
Row 1: Ch 3, 6 dc in ring, (ch 2, 7 dc in ring) 3 times, ch 2, end sl st in 3rd st of beg ch.
Row 2: Ch 3, * ch 5, 3 dc, ch 3, 3 dc, repeat from * around, end 2 dc, sl st in 3rd st of beg ch.

Row 3: Ch 3, 1 sc, ch 3, at ch-5 previous row.
Rows 4-12: Work as for rows 2-3, increasing at corners as shown.
Row 13: 1 sc, * ch 3, 2 dc in ch-5, ch 2, 2 dc in same ch as last 2 dc, ch 3, 1 sc, repeat from * around, working corners same as before.
Row 14: Work "(1 dc, 3-ch p) 4 times, 1 dc" in ch-2 (in ch-3 at corners).
From 2nd motif, work p on last row joining to previous motif with sl st as shown. Make 12 rows of 8 motifs.

Sts of Motifs & Joining

motif 96 pieces

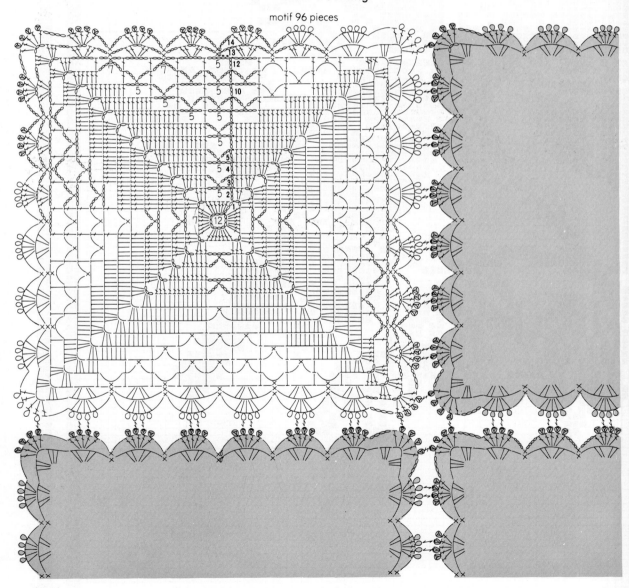

62

22 Bedspread

shown on pages 42 - 43

You'll Need:
Crochet cotton DMC #3, 509 20-g. balls White. Steel crochet hook size 1.60 mm.
Finished Size: 249 cm by 270 cm
Size of Motif: A = 21 cm in diameter B = 9 cm in diameter
Gauge: 1 row of tr = 1.1 cm
Making Instructions:
A-motif: Ch 10, sl st in 1st ch to form ring.
Rnd 1: Ch 1, 20 sc in ring, sl st in 1st ch.
Rnd 2: Sc in each sc around.
Rnd 3: Alternate 1 sc, ch 1.
Rnds 4-5: Work tr and ch referring to chart.
Rnd 6: 1 sc, ch 3, 3 3-ch p (sl st in 1st st of every p), ch 3, repeat in same way around. End off.
Rnd 7: Join cotton in where indicated, ch 1, (sc in middle p, ch 7) 20 times, end sl st in 1st ch.
Rnd 8: Sc in each st around.
Rnds 9-15: Work variation of sc increasing where indicated, snip off.

Chart on Measurements

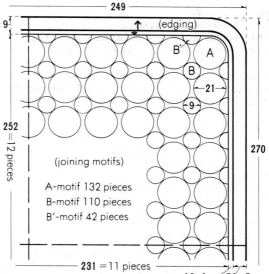

(joining motifs)

A-motif 132 pieces
B-motif 110 pieces
B'-motif 42 pieces

A-Motif

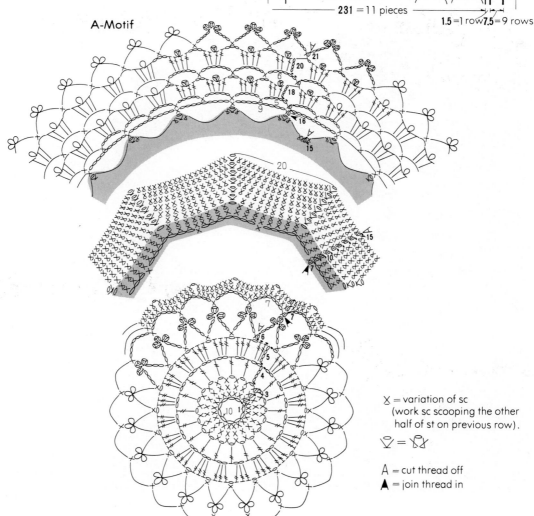

$\underline{X}$ = variation of sc
(work sc scooping the other half of st on previous row).

$\vee$ = $\curlyvee$

A = cut thread off
▲ = join thread in

Rnd 16: Join cotton in. Work ch-9 lp 20 times, tucking the surplus previous rnds.
Rnd 17: Work ch-5 lp 40 times.
Rnd 18: Work "1 tr, 1 dc, 3-ch p, 1 dc, 1 tr" in lp, ch 2, repeat in same way arond, end working 1 hdc, instead of ch 2.
Rnd 19: Alternate 1 sc, ch 6.
From 2nd motif, work p on last rnd joining to previous motif with sl st. Make 12 rows of 11 motifs.
Rnd 20: Work as for rnd 18.
Rnd 21: Work as for rnd 6.
B-motif: Work as for A-motif until 6th rnd. Work rnd 6 joining to A-motif as shown.

B'-motif: Make half of B-motif referring to chart. Work p on rnd 6 joining to A-motif as shown.
Edging: Ch 3616, sl st in 1st ch to make round.
Row 1: Dc in each st around.
Row 2: Work 1 dc, ch 1, alternately around.
Row 3: 4 dc, ch 4, 9 sc, ch 4, repeat in same way around.
Rows 4-8: Work as for previous row. Make patterns increasing dc at the dc of each pattern.
Row 9: 1 sc, ch 4, (1 dc, 3-ch p, ch 1) 8 times, 1 dc, ch 4, repeat in same way around.
Join cotton in base ch where indicated, work ch and p joining to the edge of joined-motif.

Joining Motifs & Edging

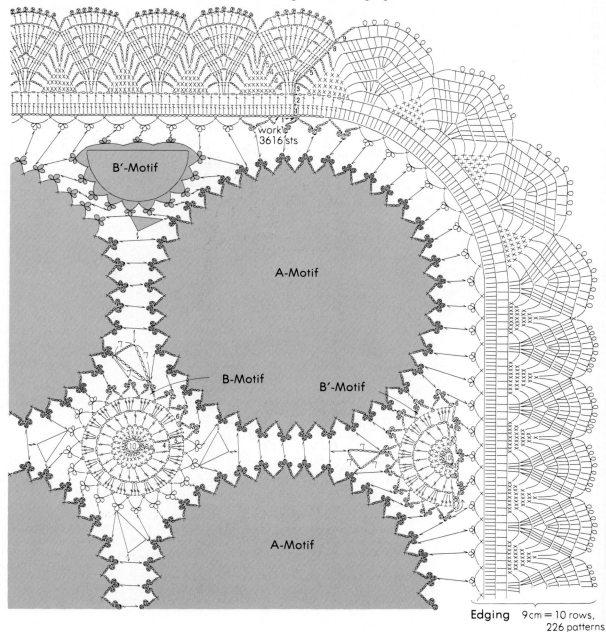

Edging 9cm = 10 rows, 226 patterns

CENTERPIECES & DOILIES

26
Instructions
on page 73

27
Instructions
on page 74

28

Instructions on page 76

29

Instructions on page 77

67

30

Instructions on page 79

31

Instructions on page 78

32

Instructions on page 79

33

Instructions on page 81

34

Instructions on page 82

35

Instructions on page 82

36

Instructions on page 84

37

Instructions on page 85

38

Instructions on page 122

26 Centerpiece

shown on page 65

You'll Need:
Crochet cotton DMC #5, 6.5 20-g. balls Beige. Steel crochet hook size 1.50 mm.
Finished Size: 70 cm by 39 cm

Gauge: Pattern crochet (1): 38 sts = 10 cm 11.5 rows = 10 cm
Pattern crochet (2): 1 row of tr = 1.1 cm

② Pattern Crochet

① Pattern Crochet

17 = work 61 ch

73

Making Instructions:
Pattern crochet (1): Ch 61. Row 1: Ch 3, dc in 5th ch from hook, dc in each of 59 sts.
Row 2: Turn, ch 3, 3 dc, (ch 3, sk 2 sts, 1 sc, ch 3, sk 2 sts, 1 dc) 9 times, end 3 dc.
Row 3: Turn, alternate ch 5, dc in dc, working dc on both sides of the row.
Rows 4-57: Repeat rows 2-3.
Row 58: Work filet crochet of ch 2, 1 dc, across.
Row 59: Dc in each st across.
Pattern crochet (2): Work along the edge of pattern crochet (1). Row 1: Work filet crochet, continued from the end of pattern crochet (1).
Row 2: Work 2-tr puff and ch at pineapple pattern as shown, work 3 sc and ch 4 for the rest.
Row 3: Where pineapple pattern is formed, work 8 dc in ch-5, "2-tr puff, ch 2, 2-tr puff" in ch-2.
Rows 4-12: Work pineapple pattern referring to chart. From row 8, make fan shape pattern between, working tr and ch as shown. Secure each p with sc.

Chart on Measurements

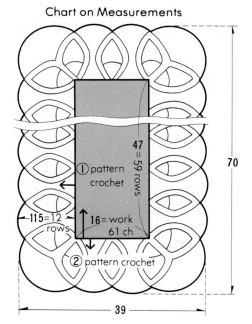

27 Centerpiece shown on page 65

You'll Need::
Crochet cotton DMC #20, 3 20-g. balls White. Steel crochet hook size 1.00, 0.90 mm.
Finished Size: 51 cm by 38 cm in oval
Gauge: 1 row of dc (with the hook #8) = 0.5 cm
Making Instructions:
Until 7th row of the leaf-motif, use crochet hook #6, use #8 for the rest.
Leaf-motif: Ch 18, Work sc on both sides of base ch.
Rows 2-7: Work along referring to chart.

Chart on Measurements

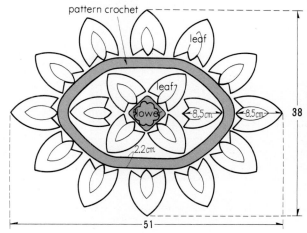

Row 8: Change hook for another, work dc and ch starting at the midway of row 7.
Row 9: Work "2 sc, ch 3, 2 dc" in each lp, making ch 2 between.
Row 10: Work as for previous row.
Row 11: 4 sc, 3-ch p, 4 sc, ch 2, 1 sc, ch 2, repeat. End off.
Make 6 pieces inside the circle, 12 pieces outside, in numerical order on the chart. From 2nd piece, work p joining to previous one.
Flower-motif: Ch 12, sl st in 1st ch to form ring.
Row 1: Ch 1, 24 sc in ring, sl st in 1st ch.
Row 2: 1 dc, ch 4, sk 2 sc, repeat.
Row 3: Work "2 sc, 3-ch p, 2 sc" in lp, ch 2, repeat. End working hdc, instead of ch 2.
Row 4: Work 1 sc, ch 6, alternately around.
Row 5: Work "1 sc, 1 hdc, 1 dc, 5 tr, 1 dc, 1 hdc, 1 sc" in each lp around.
Row 6: Work sc and ch around, making motif squarely.
Row 7: Work sc and ch, joining in the middle of 6 leaves.
Pattern crochet: Row 1: Work along the out edge of 6-leaf motif as shown.
Row 2: Work sc along.
Rows 3-5: Work dc and ch along.
Row 6: Work "2 sc, 3-ch p, 1 sc" in each ch-3 around. Work p joining to 12-leaf motif as shown.

Pattern Crochet

Leaf Motif

Flower Motif

work 18 ch

∧ = cut thread off
∧ = join thread in

75

28 Centerpiece

shown on page 66

You'll Need:
Crochet cotton DMC #20, 4 20-g. balls White. Steel crochet hook size 0.90.
Finished Size: 46 cm in diameter.
Gauge: 1 row of dc = 0.5 cm
Making Instructions:
Ch 10, sl st in 1st ch to form ring.
Rnd 1: Ch 3, 18 dc in ring, end sl st in 3rd st of beg ch.

Rnd 2: 2 dc each in each st around.
Rnd 3: Work "1 dc, ch 2, 1 dc" in every other dc.
Rnds 4-16: Work increasing sts of ch as shown.
Rnd 17: Work 8 dc in each ch-5 around.
Rnds 18-43: Make patterns working dc and ch as shown.
Rnd 44: Work "1 dc, ch 3, sc in top of dc to form p, 1 dc" at 4-dc, "ch 3, 1 sc, ch 3" at ch-4 1p.

= work in ch st.

76

29 Centerpiece

shown on page 67

You'll Need:
Crochet cotton DMC #5, 11 20-g. balls Orange.
Steel crochet hook size 1.50 mm.
Finished Size: 78 cm in diameter
Gauge: 1 row of dc = 0.7 cm
Making Instructions:
Ch 10, sl st in 1st ch to form ring.
Rnd 1: Ch 3, 19 dc in ring, sl st in 3rd st of beg ch.
Rnds 2-6: Work 2 dc increasing sts of following ch.
Rnd 7: Work as for previous rnd, making "1 dc, ch 1, 1 dc" in middle st of ch-11.
Rnds 8-14: Work making diamond pattern with dc.

Rnds 15-28: Make leaf patten of dc in same manner as for previous rnds. As for the dc on rnd 28, work in each ch between patterns.
Rnds 29-40: Work dc on top of leaf pattern as shown, making net st of ch-6 between patterns. End each rnd working ch 3, 1 dc, instead of ch 6.
Rnds 41-42: Work net st of ch-6 around.
Rnds 43-48: Make fan shape pattern in net st, working dc and ch as shown.
Rnd 49: Work sc and 3 3-ch p around, securing each of 3 p in same place with sl st.

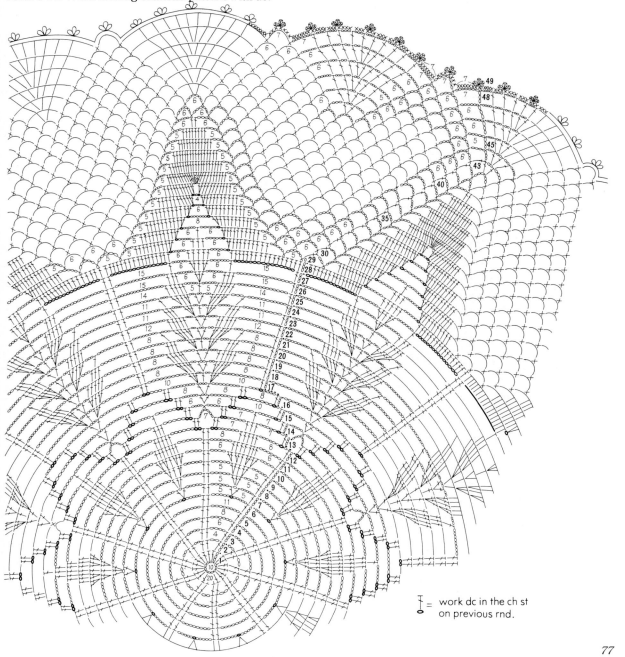

$\dagger$ = work dc in the ch st on previous rnd.

77

31 Doily shown on page 69

You'll Need:
Crochet cotton DMC #5, 3.5 20-g. balls Beige. Steel crochet hook size 1.50 mm.
Finished Size: 34 cm in diameter
Gauge: 1 row of dc = 0.9 cm
Making Instructions:
Ch 8, sl st in 1st ch to form ring.
Rnd 1: Ch 3, 23 dc in ring, end sl st in 3rd st of beg ch.
Rnd 2: Ch 6, 1 dc, ch 1, * 1 dc, ch 3, 1 dc, ch 1, repeat from * around.
Rnd 3: 7 dc each in ch-3 lp.
Rnds 4-7: Make leaf pattern increasing dc on both sides of the pattern.

Rnds 8-14: Dec dc to form leaf pattern, working net st of ch-4 between patterns.
Rnds 15-16: Work net st of ch-4 around. End each rnd working ch 2, 1 hdc, instead of ch 4.
Rnd 17: Work 1 dc, ch 4, alternately around.
Rnd 18: Work "2 dc, ch 2, 2 dc" in lp, "ch 3, 1 sc, ch 3" in next lp.
Rnd 19: Work as for previous rnd, making ch 4 between patterns.
Rnds 20-23: Work as for rnds 18-19.
Rnd 24: Work "(1 dc, 3-ch p) 5 times, 1 dc" in ch-3, "ch 3, 1 sc, ch 3" in ch-5 lp.

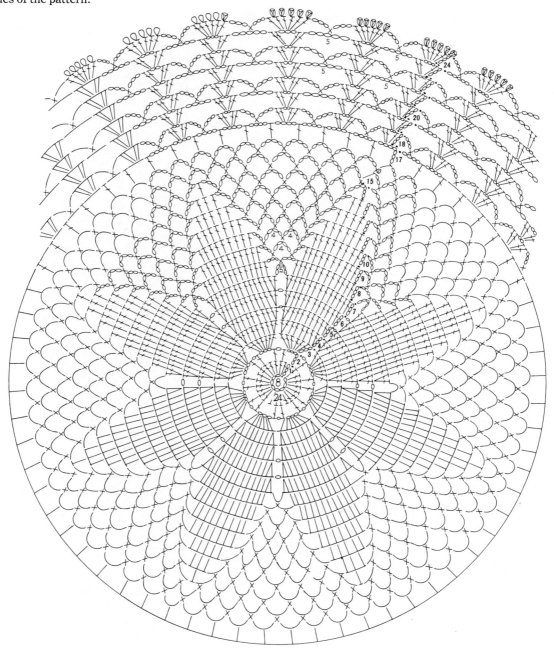

32 Doily shown on page 69

You'll Need:
Crochet cotton DMC #5, 3 20-g. balls Beige. Steel crochet hook size 1.50 mm.
Finished Size: 32 cm in diameter
Gauge: 1 row of tr = 1.3 cm
Making Instructions:
Ch 10, sl st in 1st ch to form ring.
Rnd 1: Ch 1, 20 sc in ring, sl st in 1st ch.
Rnd 2: Work 2 tr in each sc around.
Rnd 3: (3 dc, ch 4) 10 times.
Rnd 4: Work "3 tr, ch 3, 3 tr, ch 3" in each lp around.
Rnd 5: Work same as before, making ch 13 between patterns. End ch 6, 1 qtr, instead of ch 13.
Rnd 6: Work "ch 5, 1 sc, ch 5" at ch-13 lp.

Rnds 7-8: Work as for rnd 6.
Rnd 9: Alternate 10 tr in lp, ch 3.
Rnds 10-13: Work as for rnds 5-8.

30 Centerpiece shown on page 68

You'll Need:
Crochet cotton DMC #20, 6.5 20-g. balls Beige. Steel crochet hook size 0.90 mm.
Finished Size: 65 cm in diameter
Gauge: 1 row of dc = 0.5 cm
Making Instructions:
Ch 8, sl st in 1st ch to form ring.
Rnd 1: Ch 4, 2-tr puff in ring, * ch 8, 3-tr puff in ring, repeat from * 6 times, end working ch 3, 1 dtr, instead of c 8.
Rnd 2: Work "6 sc, ch 2, 6 sc" in each lp around.
Rnd 3: In ch-2 lp, make (1 dtr, ch 1) 6 times and 1 dtr.
Rnds 4-5: Work dc and ch referring to chart.
Rnds 6-8: Make patterns in same way as for previous rnd, working sc on both sides of each pattern.
Rnd 9: Make 13 sc at the pattern, ch 11 between patterns.
Rnd 10: Work sc in each st around.
Rnd 11: Work 3-dtr puff, ch 7, alternately around.
Rnd 12: Work sc around.

Rnd 13: In middle sc of each arc, make (dtr, ch 1) 5 times each.
Rnd 14: Alternate 1 dc, ch 2, to unite 2 patterns each, working 2 dc at a time at each side of the united pattern.
Rnds 15-21: Work as for rnds 5-8. Make 16 patterns.
Rnd 22: In the place between patterns, make "ch 5, 2-dtr puff in same place as ch 5, work 2 3-dtr puff at a time, inserting hook in the sc indicated, ch 5, 2-dtr puff in same place as last ch 5".
Rnd 23: Work 7 sc at the pattern of dc, ch 7, 3-tr puff, ch 5, 3-tr puff, ch 7, between patterns.
Rnds 24-32: Work as for rnds 10-12.
Rnd 33: In middle sc of each arc, make (dtr, ch 1) 3 times each. Make 96 patterns.
Rnds 34-51: Counting 4 patterns of rnd 33 as 1 pattern, make 24 patterns in same manner as for rnds 14-32.
Rnds 52-62: Work as for rnds 33-43. Make 32 patterns.
Rnds 63-64: Make 128 lps as shown.

the thickened sts in the chart skipped following rnd.

Λ = 3 sc at a time. Λ = 2 sc at a time.

33 Doily   shown on page 70

You'll Need:
Crochet cotton DMC #15, 2 20-g. balls White. Steel
crochet hook size 1.25 mm.
Finished Size: 36 cm in diameter
Gauge: 1 row of dc = 0.7 cm
Making Instructions:
Ch 16: sl st in 1st ch to form ring.
Rnd 1: Ch 1, 32 sc in ring, sl st in 1st ch.
Rnd 2: 3 dc, (ch 1, 1 dc) 2 times, ch 1, repeat.
Rnds 3-8: Work as for rnd 2, increasing dc one
side.
Rnd 9: Referring to chart, work 3-dc puff, ch 3,
alternately around.

Rnd 10: 4 sc (5 sc at 6 places) in each lp around.
Rnd 11: 3 tr at a time, ch 5, 3 tr at a time, repeat.
Rnd 12: Work net st of 1 sc, ch-7, around.
Rnd 13: Work 1 dc, ch 7, alternately around.
Rnd 14: 4 sc in lp, 3-ch p, 4 sc in same lp as before,
ch 1, repeat in same way around.
Rnd 15: Work 1 dc, ch 9, alternately around.
Rnd 16: 12 sc in each lp.
Rnds 17-24: Work dc and ch referring to chart.
Rnd 25: Work net st of 1 sc, ch-9, around, end making
ch 4, 1 dtr, instead of ch 9.
Rnd 26: Work net st of 1 sc, ch-10, around.

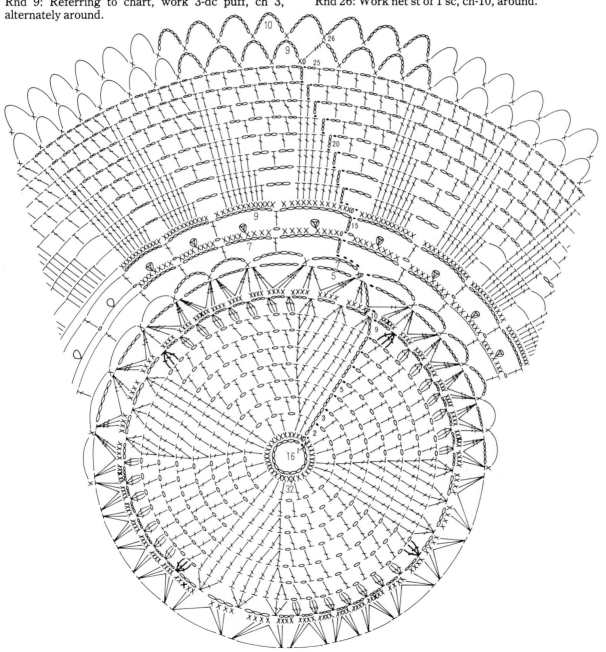

35 Doily shown on page 71

You'll Need:
Crochet cotton DMC #3, 2 20-g. balls Beige. Crochet
hook size 2.0.mm.
Finished Size: 23 cm in diameter
Gauge: 1 row of tr = 1.4 cm
Making Instructions:
Ch 8, sl st in 1st ch to form ring.
Rnd 1: Ch 5, (1 tr, ch 1) 15 times in ring, end sl st in
4th st of beg ch.
Rnd 2: Work 1 dc, ch 2, alternately around.
Rnd 3: Work net st of ch-5 around, end making ch
2, 1 dc, instead of ch 5.

Rnd 4: Work "1 tr, ch 1, 1 tr, ch 3" in middle st of
each lp.
Rnd 5: Dc in dc, ch 2, dc in dc, ch 2, sc in ch-3, ch 2,
repeat.
Rnd 6: Work 1 dc, ch 3, alternately around.
Rnd 7: Work "5 tr, ch 3" every other lp.
Rnd 8: 5 tr at a time at the tr, ch 3, crossed dc, ch 3,
at the lp following.
Rnd 9: 1 sc, ch 3, 1 sc, at the 5-tr; ch 4, 1 dc, ch 2,
1 dc, ch 4, at the lps following.
Rnd 10: 1 sc, ch 3, 1 hdc, ch 3, 1 sc in last hdc, (1 dc,
ch 3, 1 sc in last dc) 3 times, 1 hdc, ch 3, repeat.

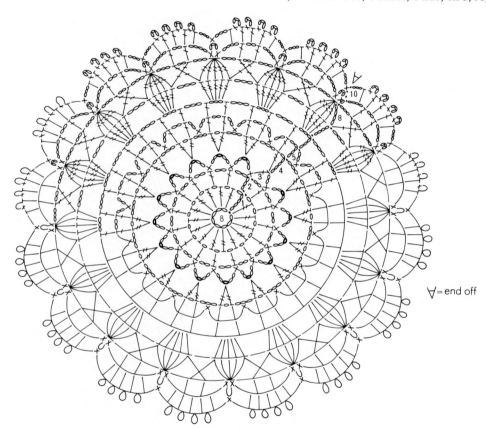

∀ = end off

34 Doily shown on page 70

You'll Need:
Crochet cotton DMC #15, 2.5 20-g. balls White,
Steel crochet hook size 1.00 mm. 14 cm square of
White linen.
Finished Size: 46 cm in diameter
Gauge: 1 row of tr = 1 cm
Making Instructions:
Filet crochet: Ch 195, sl st in 1st ch to form ring.
Row 1: Ch 1, sc in each ch (195 sts), sl st in 1st ch.
Row 2: Work filet crochet of "1 dc, ch 3" around.
Make 65 sps. End off.
Motif: Ch 6, sl st in 1st ch to form ring.

Rnd 1: Ch 5, (1 dc, ch 2) 5 times in ring, sl st in 3rd st
of beg ch.
Rnd 2: Work "(1 dc, ch 2) 2 times, 1 dc" in each dc.
Rnd 3: Work net st of ch-5, joining to filet crochet
as shown.
From 2nd motif, work last rnd joining to adjacent
sides.
Make 13 motifs around the filet crochet.
Pattern crochet: Rnd 1: Work sts of tr, ch, sc, along
the out edge of joined-motif as shown.
Rnd 2: 1 tr, 3-ch p, 1 tr, repeat referring to chart.

Rnd 3: Skipping 4 p as shown, work 4 tr between 2 dc, ch 6.
Skip 5 p at one place around.
Rnd 4: Work tr and ch 6, making 3-ch p on 3rd tr.
Rnds 5-11: Work as for previous rnd, increasing sts of ch as shown.

Rnd 12: 1 sc, 3-ch p, 1 tr, ch 2, 3-ch p, ch 1, 1 tr, 1 tr, ch 1, 3-ch p, ch 2, 1 tr, 3-ch p, 1 sc, ch 7, repeat in same way around.
Finishing: Make a linen piece of 12.5 cm in diameter, put 1st row of lace over, join steady.

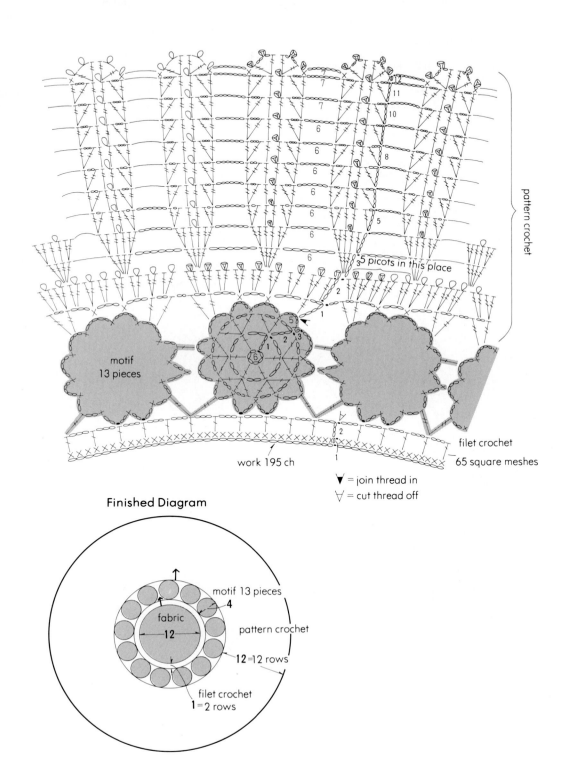

pattern crochet

5 picots in this place

motif
13 pieces

filet crochet
65 square meshes

work 195 ch

▼ = join thread in
∀ = cut thread off

Finished Diagram

motif 13 pieces
4
fabric
12
pattern crochet
12 = 12 rows
filet crochet
1 = 2 rows

36 Doily
shown on page 71

You'll Need:
Crochet cotton DMC #3, 2.5 20-g. balls Beige. Steel crochet hook size 1.75 mm.
Finished Size: 25 cm in diameter
Gauge: 1 row of dc = 0.8 cm
Making Instructions:
Ch 16: sl st in 1st ch to form ring.
Rnd 1: Ch 1, 32 sc in ring, sl st in 1st ch.
Rnd 2: Ch 5, sk 1 sc, (1 dc, ch 2, sk 1 sc) 15 times, sl st in 3rd st of beg ch.
Rnd 3: 3-tr puff in lp, ch 4, repeat.
Rnd 4: Work "1 sc, 1 hdc, 3 dc, 1 hdc, 1 sc" in each lp around.

Rnd 5: Work net st of ch-7 referring to chart, end working ch 3, 1 tr, instead of ch 7.
Rnd 6: 1 dc, ch 8, repeat.
Rnd 7: 6 dc in lp, ch 2 between lps.
Rnd 8: 1 hdc in 4th dc, ch 4, 2 dc in ch-2, ch 4, repeat.
Rnd 9: 1 hdc in lp, ch 6, repeat.
Rnd 10: Work as for rnd 7.
Rnd 11: 10 sc at the dc, ch 3, 1 dc, ch 2, 1 dc, ch 3, at the lp following.
Rnds 12-14: Work as for previous rnd.
Rnd 15: 2 sc, ch 7, "2 sc" each in ch-1 following, making 4-ch p on every 3rd sc (1st sc at the beg of each pattern).

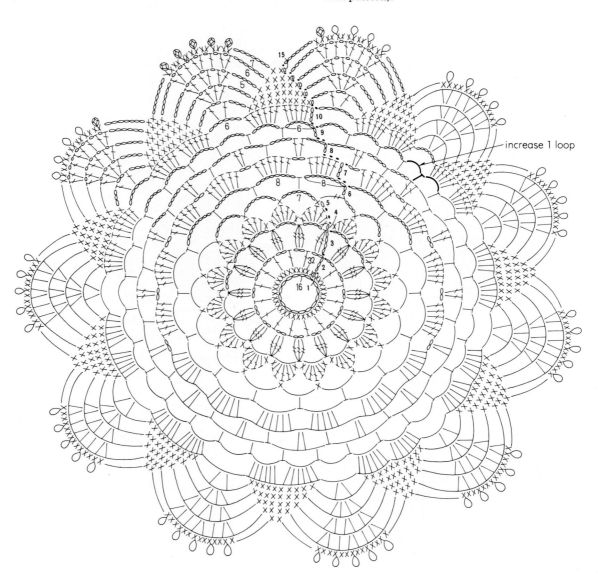

increase 1 loop

37 Doily shown on page 71

You'll Need:
Crochet cotton DMC #15, 1 20-g. ball White. Steel crochet hook size 1.00 mm.
Finished Size: 18 cm in diameter
Gauge: 1 row of dc = 0.6 cm

Making Instructions:
Ch 9, sl st in 1st ch to form ring.
Rnd 1: Ch 3, 26 dc in ring, sl st in 3rd st of beg ch.
Rnd 2: 2 dc, ch 3, sk 1 dc, repeat.
Rnds 3-9: Referring to chart, work dc and ch making 1 dc each in indicated ch.
Rnd 10: 4 dc in dc, ch 7, 7 sc in ch-5, ch 7, repeat.
Rnds 11-13: Work as for rnd 10.
Rnd 14: Work sc around, making 3-ch p on the sc indicated.

$\overline{\underset{\circ}{\rule{0pt}{12pt}}}$ = work dc in the ch st on previous rnd.

48 Border

shown on page 96

You'll Need:
Crochet cotton DMC #15, White. Steel crochet hook size 1.00 mm.

Finished Size: 14.5 cm in width.

Gauge: 1 row of dc = 0.7 cm 5 rows of ridge st = 1 cm

Making Instructions:

Motif: Ch 21. Row 1: Turn, ch 11, work "1 dtr, ch 10, 1 dtr" in the middle of base ch, ch 11, sl st in 1st st of base ch.

Row 2: 17 sc, ch 2, 17 sc.

Rows 3-20: Work ridge st referring to chart. End off. Join cotton in the lp 3rd to 4th row, work 6 rows of net st on 3 sides as shown, making p on last row where indicated.

From 2nd motif, stitch joining to previous one as shown.

Join required pieces.

Edging: Row 1: Work ch and dc or tr along the top of joined-motif making edges even.

Rows 2-3: Work dc and ch referring to chart.

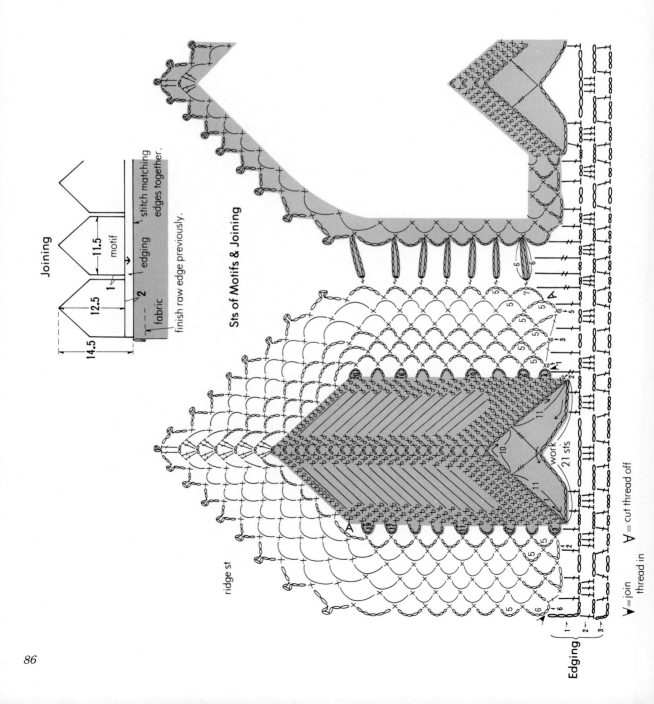

49 Border shown on page 96

You'll Need:
Crochet cotton DMC #20, White. Steel crochet hook
size 1.00 mm.
Finished Size: 20.7 cm in width
Gauge: 1 pattern = 5 cm 12 rows (1 pattern) = 4 cm
Making Instructions:
Ch 93. Row 1: Ch 1, sc in each st of the base ch.
Row 2: Turn, Ch 7, sk 2 sc, 1 dc, (ch 4, sk 2 sc, 1 dc)
2 times, ch 6, sk 4 sc, 1 sc, (ch 3, sk 1 sc, sc in sc) 6
times, ch 6, sk 4 sc, 1 dc, continue in same manner.
Rows 3-14: Make diamond patterns working net st
of ch-4 in same way as for row 2.
Repeat rows 3-14 (count as 1 pattern) until the length
of border fits to the fabric to be applied on. Snip off.
Join cotton in, work 2 rows of edging.
Apply fabric edge (folded twice to wrong side) on the
edge of lace as shown, stitch steady.

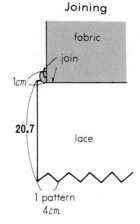

Joining

fabric

join

1cm

20.7

lace

1 pattern
4cm

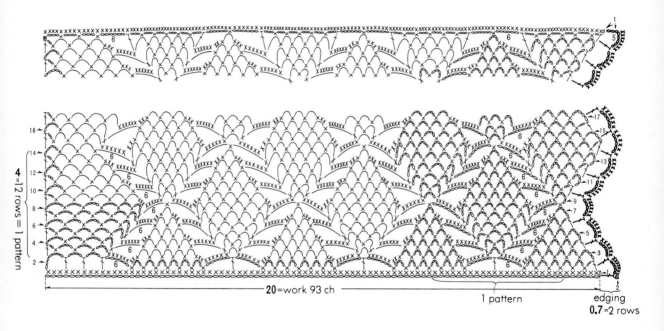

4 = 12 rows = 1 pattern

20 = work 93 ch

1 pattern

edging
0.7 = 2 rows

50 Border shown on page 96

You'll Need:
Crochet cotton DMC #20, White. Steel crochet hook
size 0.90 mm.
Finished Size: 11 cm in width
Gauge: 1 row of dc = 0.5 cm

Making Instructions:
Ch 68. Row 1: Ch 3, 1 dc, ch 2, (3 dc, ch 1) 8 times,
12 dc, (ch 1, 3 dc) 5 times.
Row 2: Turn, ch 2, work "3 dc, ch 1" in each ch,
making pattern of dc shifting 2 sts as shown.
Rows 3-10: Work as for row 2, decreasing one side as
shown.
Rows 12-19: Work increasing one side.
Repeat rows 2-19 (count as 1 pattern) required times.
Apply lace on the edge of fabric, stitch steady.

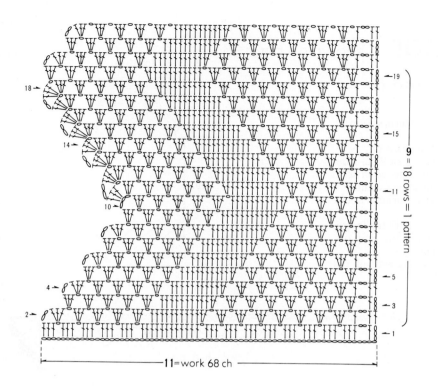

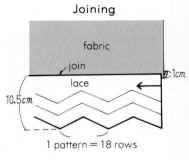

Joining

fabric

join

lace

10.5cm

1 pattern = 18 rows

9 = 18 rows = 1 pattern

11=work 68 ch

51 Border shown on page 96

You'll Need:
Crochet cotton DMC #20, White. Steel crochet hook size 0.90 mm.

Finished Size: 10.5 cm in width

Gauge: 1 row of dc = 0.5 cm

Making Instructions:
Ch 45. Row 1: Ch 3, 2 dc, (ch 5, sk 5 sts, 1 dc) 7 times.
Row 2: Turn, ch 5, 7 dc, (ch 3, 1 sc, ch 3, 1 dc) 5 times, 2 dc.
Row 3: Work as for 1st row.
Row 4: Ch 4, 3-ch p, (1 tr, 3-ch p) 2 times, 1 tr. Work following sts in same way as for row 2.
Rows 5-10: Work as for rows 3-4, increasing one side as shown.
Rows 11-15: Work decreasing one side.
Repeat rows 2-15 (count as 1 pattern) required times. Place lace edge over the lace, stitch steady.

Joining

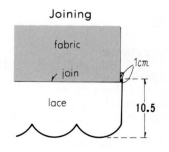

fabric

join

lace

1cm

10.5

place over the fabric, stitch steady

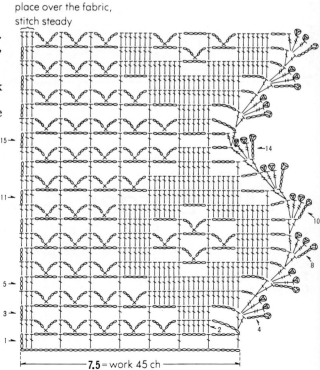

7.5 = 14 rows = 1 pattern

7.5 = work 45 ch

PILLOWS

39
Instructions on page 97

Instructions on page 98

Instructions on page 99

42
Instructions on page 100

43

Instructions on page 102

44

Instructions on page 103

45

Instructions on page 104

46
Instructions on page 105

47
Instructions on page 106

BORDERS

Instructions
on page 86—88

48

49

50

51

39 Pillow

shown on page 89

You'll Need:

Crochet cotton DMC #5, 21 20-g. balls White. Steel crochet hook size 1.25mm. Cotton satin Navy Blue 58cm by 116cm for innercase. 500-g. kapok.

Finished Size: 55cm in diameter

Gauge: 1 row of tr = 0.9cm

Making Instructions:

Ch 12, sl st in 1st ch to form ring.

Rnd 1: Ch 1, 24 sc in ring, sl st in 1st ch.

Rnd 2: Ch 3, (dc in sc) 23 times, sl st in 3rd st of beg ch.

Rnd 3: Work net st of ch-5 around, end working ch 2, 1 dc, instead of ch 5.

Rnd 4: Net st of ch-7 around, end working ch 3, 1 tr.

Rnd 5: Work "2 tr, ch 2, 2 tr" in middle st of ch-7, ch 3, repeat.

Rnds 6-14: Make 12 patterns of diamond working tr as shown.

From rnd 11, make new pattern between diamonds.

Rnds 15-28: Make shell st on top of each diamond, working tr and ch as shown. From rnd 19, work pineapple pattern in 12 places.

Rnd 29: Work 1 sc, ch 7, alternately around. End off.

Make 2 pieces for front and back, join stitching 1 sc, ch 5, zigzag as shown. Insert inner-case at the midway of joining.

Inner-case: Sew the case of 55cm in diameter, stuff kapok previously.

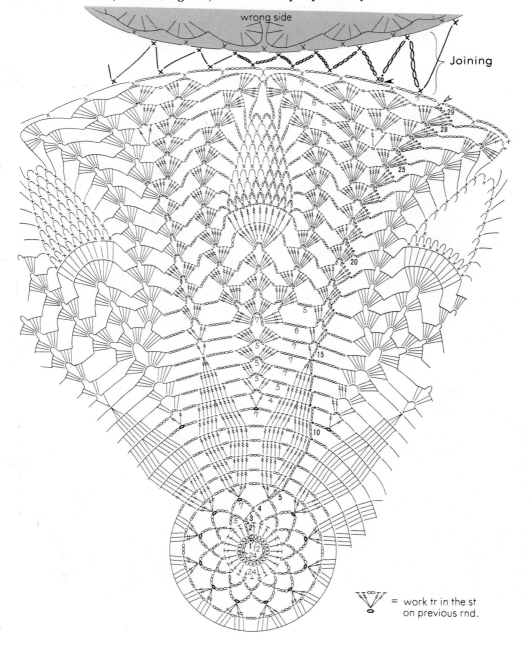

= work tr in the st on previous rnd.

40 Pillow   shown on page 90

You'll Need:
Crochet cotton DMC #5, 9.5 20-g. balls (for each)
White. Steel crochet hook size 1.25 mm. Bemberg for
inner-case 72 cm by 49 cm each of Red, Navy Blue.
500-g. kapok (for each).
Finished Size: 46 cm by 34.5 cm
Size of Motif: A = 11.5 cm in diameter B = 4 cm in
diameter
Gauge: 1 row of dc = 0.7 cm
Making Instructions:
A-motif: Ch 12, sl st in 1st ch to form ring.

Row 1: Ch 3, 35 dc in ring, sl st in 3rd st of beg ch.
Row 2: 1 dc (ch 3 at the beg), ch 11, 12 dc in ch-11 just
worked, making 2 dc in same st at the beg. Dc in
1st row, skipping 2 sts of dc, ch 10. Dc in 6th dc
(from center) of the 12 dc worked before, make 3 sps
working ch 2, 1 dc, alternately. Ch 5, turn, make
2 sps of filet crochet referring to chart, work 12 dc.
Make 12 patterns in same manner.
Row 3: Work sc along filet crochet and ch-5, making
4-ch p at the middle of ch-5.
From 2nd motif, work last rnd joining to previous
motif reffering to chart, and leaving the opening for
stuffing.

Sts of Motifs & Joining

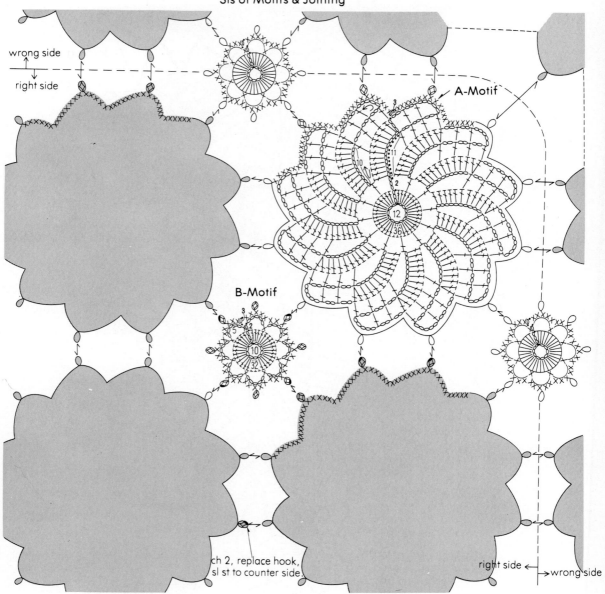

wrong side
right side

A-Motif

B-Motif

ch 2, replace hook,
sl st to counter side.

right side ← →wrong side

B-motif: Ch 10, sl st in 1st ch to form ring.
Rnd 1: Ch 3, 31 dc in ring, sl st in 3rd st of beg ch.
Rnd 2: Make 8 lps of ch-5, skipping 3 dc each.
Rnd 3: 5 sc in each lp, making 4-ch p on middle sc.
Work p joining to adjacent motifs as shown.
Inner-case: Make 46cm by 34.5cm oblong case corners rounded, stuff kapok previously.

Chart on Measurements

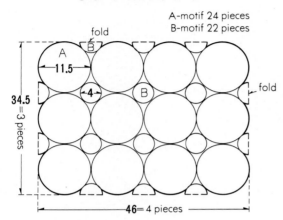

A-motif 24 pieces
B-motif 22 pieces

41 Pillow   shown on page 91

You'll Need:
Crochet cotton DMC #15, 8.5 20-g. balls (for each) White. Steel crochet hook size 1.00mm. Bemberg for inner-case 51cm by 99cm each of Red, Navy Blue. 650-g. kapok. (for each).
Finished Size: 48cm square
Size of Motif: 12cm square
Gauge: 1 row of dc = 0.6cm
Making Instructions:
Motif: Ch 8, sl st in 1st ch to form ring.
Rnd 1: Ch 3, 23 dc in ring, sl st in 3rd st of beg ch.
Rnd 2: 4 dc, ch 2, repeat referring to chart.
Rnds 3-9: Make patterns working dc and net st of ch-5. Work rnd 9 making "3-dc puff, ch 3, 3-dc puff" at each corner.
End each rnd working ch 2, 1 dc, instead of ch 5.
Rnds 10-11: Work as for previous rnd, making 5-ch p on the corner sc of rnd 11.
From 2nd motif, work last rnd joinig to previous motif. Make 2 pieces of 4 motifs by 4 motifs, join together leaving the opening for stuffing, put inner-case into, stitch closed.
Inner-case: Make 48cm square bemberg case, each in Red, Navy Blue, stuff kapok previously.

Chart on Measurements
motif 32 pieces (right side, wrong side 16 pieces each)

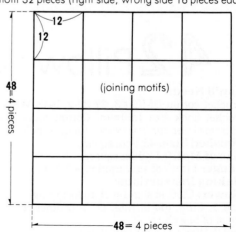

42 Pillow shown on page 92

You'll Need:
Crochet cotton DMC #3, 27 20-g. balls White. Steel crochet hook size 1.50 mm. Cotton broad 90 cm by 46.5 cm Green for inner case. 450-g. kapok.
Finished Size: 43.5 cm square
Size of Motif: 14.5 cm square
Gauge: 4 rows of sc (variation) = 1.5 cm
Making Instructions:
Flower: Ch 6, sl st in 1st ch to form ring.
Rnd 1: Ch 6, (dc in ring, ch 3) 5 times, end sl st in 3rd st of beg ch.
Rnd 2: Work "1 sc, 1 hdc, 2 dc, 1 hdc, 1 sc" in each lp around.
Rnd 3: Work sc in wrong side of the dc on 1st rnd, ch 5, repeat. Make 6 lps.

Rnd 4: Work "1 sc, 1 hdc, 4 dc, 1 hdc, 1 sc" in each lp around.
Rnds 5-6: Work as for rnds 3-4.
Make 18 pieces in same manner.
Leaf: Ch 13. Row 1: Ch 1, 13 sc, ch 2, 13 sc in counter side as shown.
Rows 2-10: Work variation of sc referring to chart.
Make 3 pieces in same manner.
As for the 4th piece, work same as before until 10th row, work 11th row joining to previous 3 pieces as shown.
Row 12: Work sc and ch along the out edge of joined-leaf referring to chart.
Work sc and p in each lp around.

Joining motifs: From 2nd motif, work row 13 joining to previous motif. Make 2 pieces of 3 motifs by 3 motifs for front and back. Join front and back putting inner-case into. Secure 18 flowers 1 each in the middle of each motif.

Inner-case: Saw 43.5 cm square case, stuff kapok previously.

Chart on Measurements

motif 18 pieces (right side, wrong side 9 pieces each)

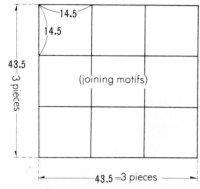

Sts of Flower Motifs

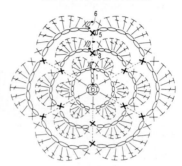

sc at 3 & 5 rows stitch in wrong side of before previous raw.

Sts of Leaf Motifs & Joining

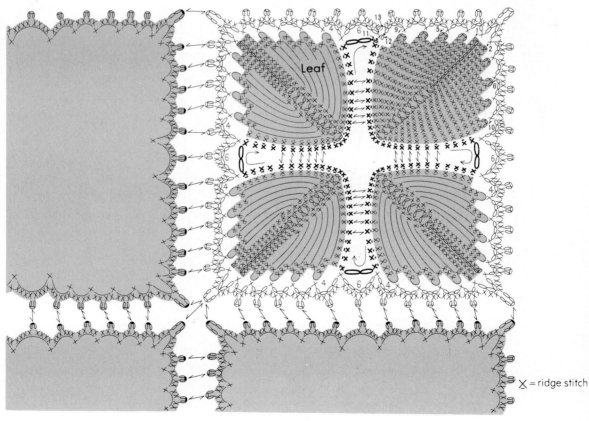

Leaf

X = ridge stitch

43 Pillow

shown on page 93

You'll Need:
Crochet cotton DMC #4, 3.5 50-g. balls Orange.
Crochet hook size 2.30 mm. Bemberg 83 cm by 42 cm
Blue for inner-case. 300-g. kapok.
Finished Size: 40.5 cm in diameter Fringe 4 cm long
Gauge: 1 row of tr = 1.7 cm
Making Instructions:
Ch 15, sl st in 1st ch to form ring.
Rnd 1: Ch 3, 29 dc in ring, sl st in 3rd st of beg ch.
Rnd 2: Work net st of ch-5 around, end with ch 2,
1 dc, instead of ch 5.
Rnds 3-4: Work net st increasing sts of ch.

Rnd 5: Work "3 tr, ch 3, 3 tr" in lp, ch 7, sc in next lp,
ch 7, repeat.
Rnds 6-14: Make 5 patterns referring to chart.
Rnds 15-16: Net st of ch-7 around.
Rnd 17: 7 sc in each lp around.
Make 2 pieces in same manner.
Edging: Put 2 pieces wrong sides together, join
with 1 row of sc around, working sc only in top piece
for about 10 arcs to make an opening for stuffing. Work
fringe in each sc around.
Make 39 cm diameter inner-case, insert into, stitch
opening closed.

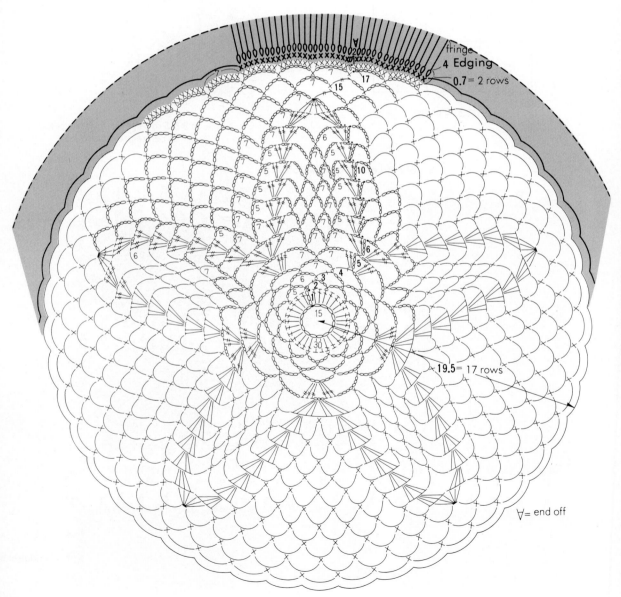

19.5 = 17 rows

∀ = end off

102

44 Pillow shown on page 93

You'll Need:
Crochet cotton DMC #4, 5 50-g. balls Sage Green.
Crochet hook size 2.30 mm. Bemberg 90 cm by 45 cm
Yellow for inner-case. 350-g. kapok.
Finished Size: 44.5 cm in diameter Fringe 4 cm long
Gauge: 1 row of dc = 1 cm
Making Instructions:
Ch 12, sl st in 1st ch to form ring.
Rnd 1: Ch 3, 23 dc in ring, sl st in 3rd st of beg ch.
Rnd 2: (1 sc, ch 5) 8 times.

Rnd 3: Work "(1 dc, ch 1) 3 times, 1 dc" in lp, ch 2, repeat.
Rnds 4-21: Make 8 patterns increasing sts as shown. Make 2 pieces in same manner.
Edging: Put 2 pieces wrong sides together, join with 1 row of sc around. Work sc only in front piece for about 2 patterns to make opening. Work fringe in each sc around.
Make 43 cm diameter inner-case, insert into, stitch opening closed.

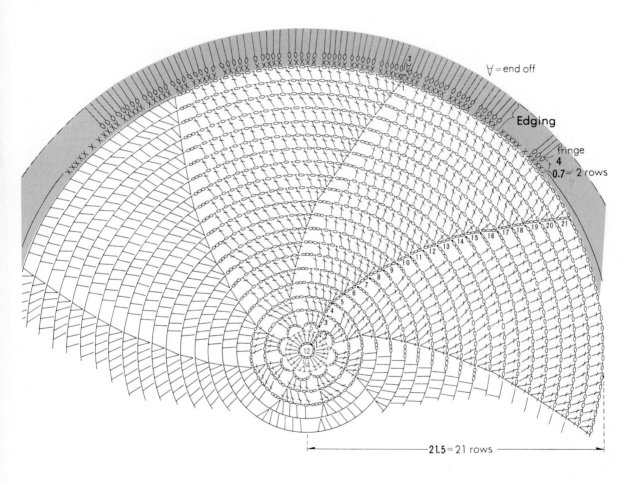

∀ = end off

Edging

fringe
4
0.7 = 2 rows

21.5 = 21 rows

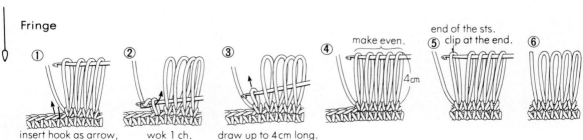

Fringe

① insert hook as arrow, draw thread through.

② wok 1 ch.

③ draw up to 4 cm long.

④ make even.

⑤ end of the sts. clip at the end.

⑥

4 cm

45 Pillow

shown on page 94

You'll Need:

Crochet cotton DMC #15, 12 20-g. balls White. Steel crochet hook size 1.00 mm. Cotton broad 49.5 cm by 96 cm each of Pink, Light Blue for inner-case. 550-g. kapok (for each).

Finished Size: 46.5 cm square
Size of Motif: 15.5 cm square
Gauge: 1 row of dc = 0.6 cm

Sts of Flower

as for the sc on 4th and 6th rnd, work in wrong side of the sc on the rnd before last, turning each petal toward you.

Sts of Motifs & Joining

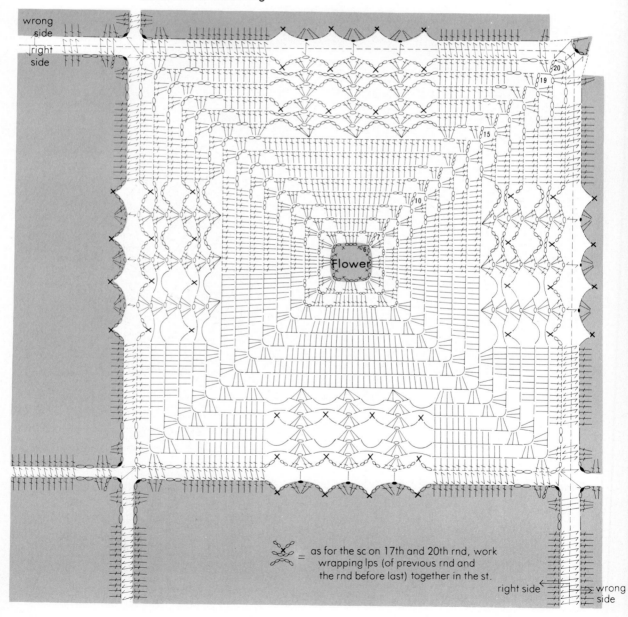

as for the sc on 17th and 20th rnd, work wrapping lps (of previous rnd and the rnd before last) together in the st.

Making Instructions:
Motif: Begin at the center of flower.
Ch 10, sl st in 1st ch to form ring. Rnd 1: Ch 1, 24 dc in ring, sl st in 1st ch.
Rnd 2: (1 sc, ch 3) 8 times.
Rnd 3: Work "1 sc, 1 hdc, 1 dc, 1 sc" in each lp around.
Rnd 4: Make 8 lps of ch-3, working sc in wrong side of the sc on 2nd rnd.
Rnd 5: Make petals working as for rnd 3.
Rnd 6: Make 8 lps of ch-3 in same way as for rnd 4.
Rnds 7-20: Work dc and ch increasing sts as shown. From 15th rnd, make patterns in each of 4 sides referring to chart.
Finishing: From 2nd motif, work last rnd making sl st to join. Join motifs pillow front and pillow back (3 pieces by 3 pieces each side) halfway referring to chart. Insert inner-case, stitch opening closed.
Inner-case: Make 46.5cm square case of broadcloth each in Pink, Light Blue, stuff kapok previously.

Chart on Measurements
motif 18 pieces (right side, wrong side 9 pieces each)

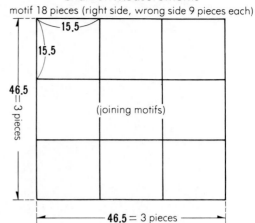

46 Pillow shown on page 95

You'll Need:
Crochet cotton DMC #20, 6.5 20-g. balls White. Steel crochet hook size 0.90mm. Cotton satin 76cm by 56cm Red for inner-case. 400-g. kapok.
Finished Size: 53cm by 36.5cm
Size of Motif: A=8.3cm in diameter B=3cm in diameter
Gauge: 1 row of dc=0.5cm
Making Instructions:
A-motif: Ch 9, sl st in 1st ch to form ring.
Rnd 1: Ch 1, 18 sc in ring, sl st in 1st ch.
Rnd 2: (1 sc, ch 3) 6 times.
Rnd 3: 5 dc in ch-3, dc in sc, repeat.
Rnds 4-6: Work dc and ch referring to chart.
Rnd 7: (1 sc, ch 8) 12 times.
Rnd 8: Work filet crochet (1 dc, ch 2) referring to chart.
Adjust the number of sps so that 20 patterns can be made on next 2 rnds.
From 2nd motif, work last rnd joining as shown. Make 2 pieces of 6 motifs by 4 motifs.
B-motif: Ch 8, sl st in 1st ch to form ring. Work sc and ch joining to A-motifs.
Edging: Make 3 rows of net st around the front piece of joined-motif, 2 rows around the back piece of joined-motif. Work 3rd row of back piece halfway joining to front.
Insert inner-case, stitch opening closed.
Inner-case: Make satin case 53cm by 36.5cm in size corners rounded, stuff kapok previously.

Chart on Measurements

A-motif 48 pieces
B-motif 30 pieces

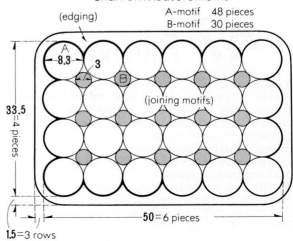

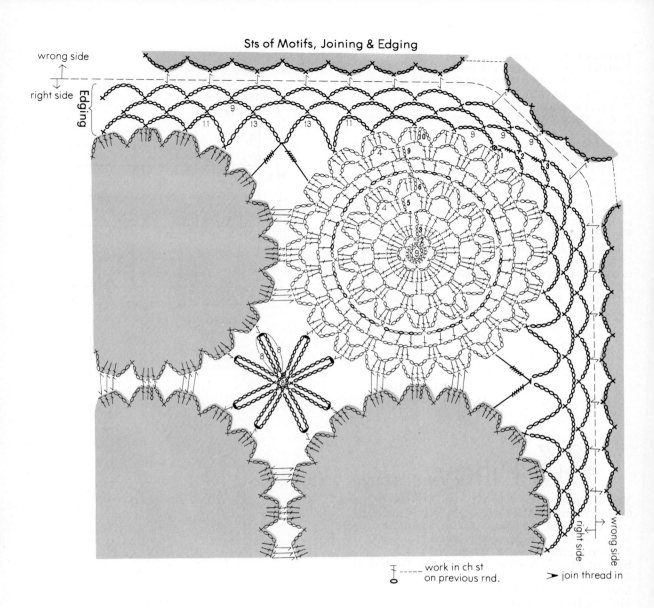

wrong side

right side

Edging

9

11   13   13   11

work in ch st
on previous rnd.

join thread in

right side

wrong side

47 Pillow   shown on page 95

You'll Need:
Crochet cotton DMC #5, 15 20-g. balls White. Steel crochet hook size 1.25 mm. Cotton satin 83 cm by 43 cm Navy Blue for inner-case. 400-g. kapok.
Finished Size: 40 cm square
Size of Motif: 12.8 cm square
Gauge: 1 row of dc = 0.6 cm
Making Instructions:
Motif: Ch 8, sl st in 1st ch to form ring.
Rnd 1: Ch 3, 19 dc in ring, sl st in 3rd st of beg ch.
Rnd 2: (1 sc, ch 7, 1 sc) 4 times.
Rnd 3: 11 tr in lp, ch 3, repeat.

Rnd 4: Work "1 tr, ch 1" at the tr, "ch 3, 1 sc, ch 3" at the lp.
Rnds 5-13: Work pineapple pattern in 4 places as shown, increasing dc and ch at 4 corners.
From 2nd motif, work joining on last rnd. Make 3 motifs by 3 motifs, trim with 1 row of edging, working dc and ch around.
Finishing: Make back piece same as for front. Work edging halfway joining to front, insert inner-case, continue edging in same way to the end.
Inner-case: Make 40 cm square satin case Navy Blue, stuff kapok previously.

106

Chart on Measurements

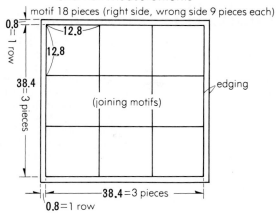

motif 18 pieces (right side, wrong side 9 pieces each)

0.8 = 1 row

12.8

12.8

38.4 = 3 pieces

(joining motifs)

edging

38.4 = 3 pieces

0.8 = 1 row

Sts of Motifs & Joining

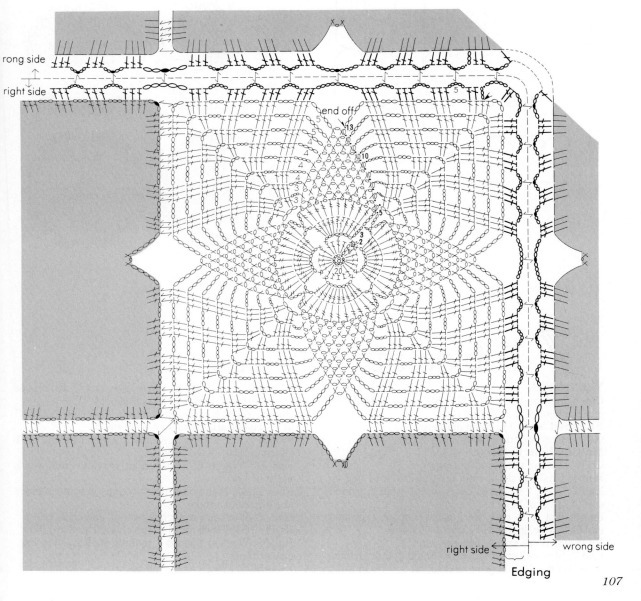

rong side

right side

end off

edging

right side

wrong side

Edging

15 Tablecloth shown on page 16

You'll Need:
Crochet cotton DMC #20, 45.5 20-g. balls White.
Steel crochet hook size 0.90 mm.
Finished Size: 168 cm by 126 cm
Size of Motif: 3.5 cm in diameter
Gauge: 2 rows of dc = 1.1 cm
Making Instructions:

Motif: Ch 8, sl st in 1st ch to form ring.
Rnd 1: Ch 1, 16 sc in ring, sl st in 1st ch.
Rnd 2: Ch 4, * dc in sc, 3-ch p, dc in next sc, ch 1, repeat from * around, end sl st in 3rd st of beg ch.
Rnd 3: Sl st in ch, ch 10, * dc in ch, ch 7, repeat from * around, sl st in 3rd st of beg ch.
Rnd 4: Ch 1, * 9 sc in ch-7 lp, 3-ch p, repeat from * around, sl st in 1st ch. End off.
From 2nd motif, work rnd 4 joining to previous motif.
Make 36 rows of 48 motifs.

Chart on Measurements

motif 1728 pieces

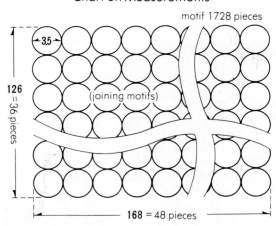

motif 1728 pieces

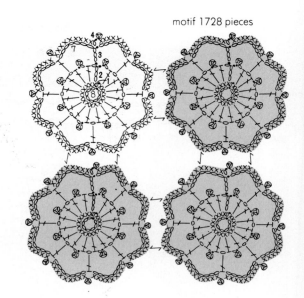

7 Tablecloth shown on page 7

You'll Need:
Crochet cotton DMC #3, 30.5 20-g. balls Beige. Steel crochet hook size 2.00 mm.
Finished Size: 112 cm in diameter.
Gauge: 1 row of dc = 1.1 cm
Making Instructions:
Ch 12, sl st in 1st ch to form ring.
Rnd 1: Ch 3, 23 dc in ring, sl st in 3rd st of beg ch.
Rnd 2: Ch 4, * dc in dc, ch 1, repeat from * around, sl st in 3rd st of beg ch.
Rnd 3: Sl st in ch, ch 1, work net st (1 sc, ch 5) around, end ch 2, 1 dc, instead of ch 5.
Rnds 4-6: Work net st of ch-5 around.
Rnd 7: Sl st in 3 sts, ch 3, dc in lp, ch 2, 2 dc in same lp as last dc, * ch 3, sc in next lp, ch 3, 2 dc in the lp

followed, ch 3, 2 dc in same lp as last 2 dc, repeat from * around, sl st in 3rd st of beg ch.
Rnd 8: Work 8 dc in ch-3, work "2 dc, ch 2, 2 dc" in ch-2 (shell st), making ch-6 between.
Rnd 9: Work shell st in shell st, repeat 1 dc and ch 1 alternately in each of 8 dc.
Rnd 10: Where at (1 dc, ch 1) previous rnd, work net st of 1 sc, ch 3.
Rnds 11-47: Make pineapple patterns in same manner as for previous rnds.
Rnd 48: Work net st of ch-6 around, end ch 3, 1 dc.
Rnds 49-54: Work net st of the ch indicated around.
Rnd 55: Work as for rnd 7, making shell st, ch 3, 1 sc, ch 3 around.
Rnds 56-57: Work as for rnd 55.

23 Bedspread

shown on pages 44 - 45

You'll Need:
Crochet cotton DMC #5, 173 20-g. balls White. Steel crochet hook sizez 1.60 mm.
Finished Size: 234 cm by 270 cm
Size of Motif: 18 cm in diameter
Gauge: 4 rows of sc = 1 cm
Making Instructions:
Motif: Ch 8, sl st in 1st ch to form ring.
Rnd 1: Ch 1, 15 sc in ring.
Rnd 2: Ch 1, (3 sc, ch 2) 5 times.
Rnds 3-20: Work sc and ch increasing sts as shown to form 5 patterns.

Rnd 21: Net st of 1 sc, ch-5, around, end working ch 2, 1 dc, instead of ch 5.
Rnds 22-25: Work net st referring to chart.
Rnd 26: Sc in each st of ch.
From 2nd motif, work last rnd making sl st where indicated to join. Make 15 rows of 13 motifs.
Open filling: Ch 12, sl st in 1st ch to form ring.
Rnd 1: Ch 1, 24 sc in ring, sl st in 1st ch.
Rnd 2: Work sc increasing at 8 places as shown.
Rnd 3: 3 sc, ch 9, sc in adjacent motif, ch 9, repeat in same way around.
Work "open filling" in 168 places.

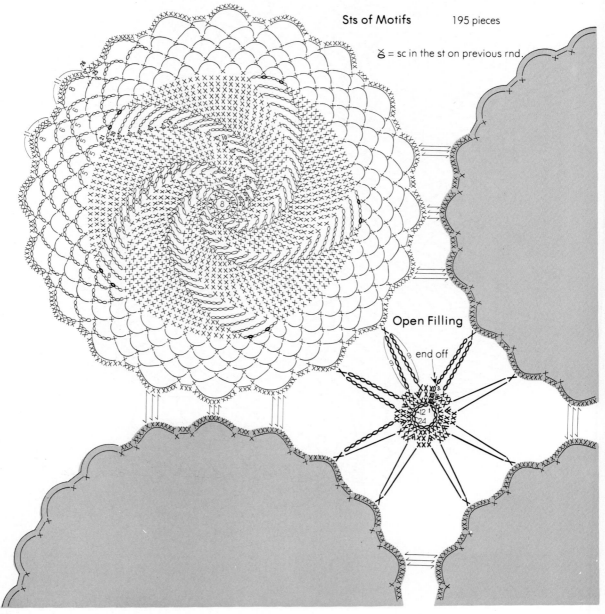

Sts of Motifs   195 pieces

⅄ = sc in the st on previous rnd.

Open Filling

end off

4 Tablecloth shown on page 4

You'll Need:
Crochet cotton DMC #5, 50 20-g. balls White. Steel crochet hook size 1.50 mm.
Finished Size: 158 cm in diameter
Gauge: 1 row of dc = 0.9 cm
Making Instructions:
Ch 8, sl st in 1st ch to form ring.
Rnd 1: Ch 1, 16 sc in ring, sl st in 1st ch.
Rnd 2: Ch 7, (tr in sc, ch 3) 15 times, sl st in 4th st of beg ch.

Rnd 3: Sl st in ch, ch 4, 4-tr puff in lp, * ch 5, 5-tr puff in next lp, repeat from * around, end ch 2, 1 dc, instead of ch 5.
Rnd 4: Ch 11, * 1 tr, ch 7, repeat from * around, end sl st in 4th st of beg ch.
Rnd 5: Ch 1, 1 sc, work net st (ch 5, 1 sc) around, end ch 2, 1 dc, instead of ch 5.
Rnd 6: Work net st of ch-7 around, end ch 3, 1 tr.
Rnd 7: Work as for rnd 4 making ch-5 lps.

Continued on Next Page

Rnd 8: Ch 3, 2 dc in same place, ch 3, 3 dc in same st as last 2 dc, work "3 dc, ch 3, 3 dc" in each tr around, end sl st in 3rd st of beg ch.

Rnd 9: Sl st in 3 sts, ch 3, work "2 dc, ch 3, 3 dc" in ch-3, ch 5, sc in next lp, ch 10, sc in the lp next, ch 5 work "3dc, ch 3, 3 dc" in lp (shell st), ch 1, continue in same way around, sl st in 3rd st of beg ch.

Rnd 10: 11 tr in ch-10 lp. Work shell st and ch referring to chart.

Rnd 11: Dc in tr, ch 1. For the rest, work as for previous rnd.

Rnd 12: Where at "1 dc, ch 1" previous rnd, work net st (ch 5, 1 sc). For the rest, work as for previous rnd.

Rnds 13-21: Work shell st and net st referring to chart.

Rnd 22: Where at shell st, work 3 dc, ch 2 between shell sts. For the rest, work ch-6 net st around.

Rnd 23: Work as for previous rnd, end ch 3, 1 dc, instead of ch 6.

Rnds 24-46: Work net st increasing sts of ch.

Rnd 47: Work shell st every 2 arcs.

Rnd 48: Sl st in 3 sts, ch 3, work "2 dc, (ch 3, 3 dc) 2 times" in ch-3 lp, ch 10, sc in next lp, ch 10, (3 dc, ch 3) 2 times, 3 dc, continue in same way around, sl st in 3rd st of beg ch.

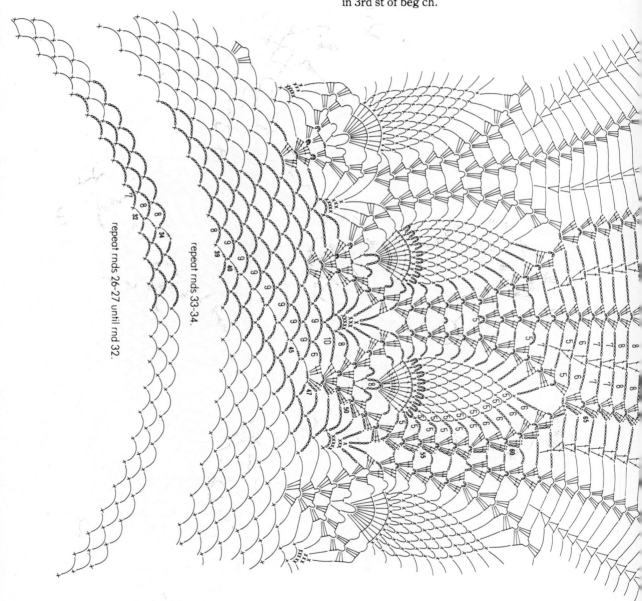

repeat rnds 26-27 until rnd 32.

repeat rnds 33-34.

Rnd 49: Work as for rnd 48.
Rnd 50: Sl st in 3 sts, ch 3, work "2 dc, ch 3, 3 dc" in ch-3, ch 5, work "1 dc, ch 8, 1 dc" in ch-2, ch 5, 1 shell st, ch 6, 5 sc in ch-4, continue in same way around, sl st in 3rd st of beg ch.
Rnds 51-62: Work as for rnds 10-21.

Rnd 63: Work as for rnd 62, making "1 dc, ch 2, 1 dc" where at 1 dc.
Rnds 64-75: "1 dc, ch 2, 1 dc" between shell sts, increasing sts of ch as shown.
Rnds 76-92: Work as for rnds 10-23, making pineapple patterns as shown.
Rnds 93-95: Work net st of ch-9 around.

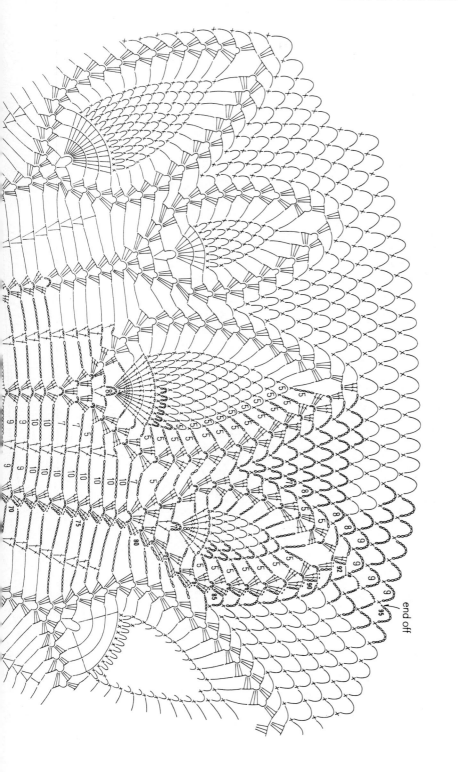

8 Tablecloth

shown on page 8, cover front

You'll Need:
Crochet cotton DMC #5, 96 20-g. balls Silver Gray.
Steel crochet hook size 1.50 mm.
Finished Size: 202 cm in diameter.
Gauge: 1 row of tr = 1 cm
Making Instructions:
Ch 15, sl st in 1st ch to form ring.
Rnd 1: Ch 3, 29 dc in ring, sl st in 3rd st of beg ch.
Rnd 2: Ch 6, * 3 dc, ch 3, repeat from * around, end
2 dc, sl st in 3rd st of beg ch.

Rnd 3: Work as for previous rnd, making ch-4 between.
Rnd 4: Dc in each of 3 dc, work (ch 2, 1 dc) 2 times, ch 2 in each of ch-4 lp.
Rnd 5: Tr in each of 3 dc, work "ch 4, 3 tr, ch 4" in each of middle ch-2.

Rnds 6-7: Work as for previous rnd, making 2 tr each in both sides of tr between lps.

Rnd 8: In the middle tr between lps previous rnd, work ch 5, 1 tr, 3-ch p, ch 5.

Rnds 9-13: Referring to chart, make diamond pattern leaving 1 st each both sides. Work tr together with p in each lp.

Rnd 14: Sl st in ch, ch 4, 2 tr in lp, ch 3, 3 tr in same lp as last tr, ch 6, sk 2 sps, tr in 3-ch p, ch 3, tr in same p, ch 6, sk 2 sps, 3 tr in lp, ch 3, 3 tr in same lp as last 3 tr, continue in same manner around, end sl st in 4th st of beg ch.

Rnds 15-35: Work as for rnds 5-13, making leaf pattern 14 times.

Rnds 36-57: Work as for rnds 14-35, making leaf pattern 28 times.

Rnds 58-79: Repeat leaf pattern 56 times.

Rnds 80-95: Repeat leaf pattern 63 times referring to chart.

Continued on Next Page

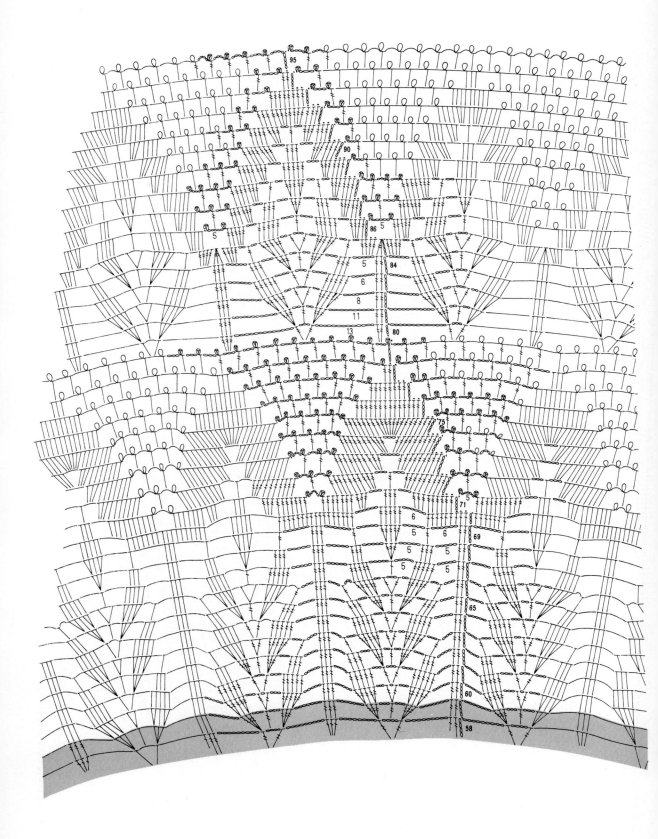

25 Bedspread

shown on page 48

You'll Need:
Crochet cotton DMC #5, 153 20-g. balls White. Steel crochet hook size 1.25 mm.
Finished Size: 215 cm by 251 cm
Size of Motif: 22 cm square
Gauge: 1 row of dc = 0.7 cm
Pattern crochet (edging): 42 sts = 10 cm 14.5 rows = 10 cm
Making Instructions:
Motif: Ch 10, sl st in 1st ch to form ring.
Row 1: Ch 3, 19 dc in ring, sl st in 3rd st of beg ch.
Row 2: Ch 3, dc in dc, ch 3, (dc in each of 2 dc, ch 3) 9 times.

Row 3: Work "2 dc, ch 4, 2 dc" in ch-3 lp.
Row 4: 9 dc in each lp around.
Row 5: Sl st in 4 sts, ch 3, dc in same place as ch-3, ch 10, * 2 dc in middle dc, ch 10, repeat from * around.
Row 6: Dc in ch, ch 2, dc in ch, ch 3, continue in same way around, end working ch 1, 1 hdc, instead of ch 3.
Row 7: 1 sc, (ch 4, 2-tr puff in 1st st of ch 4) 2 times, repeat.
Rows 8-10: Work dc and ch referring to chart.
Rows 11-15: Work dc and ch making patterns squarely.

Sts of Motifs & Joining

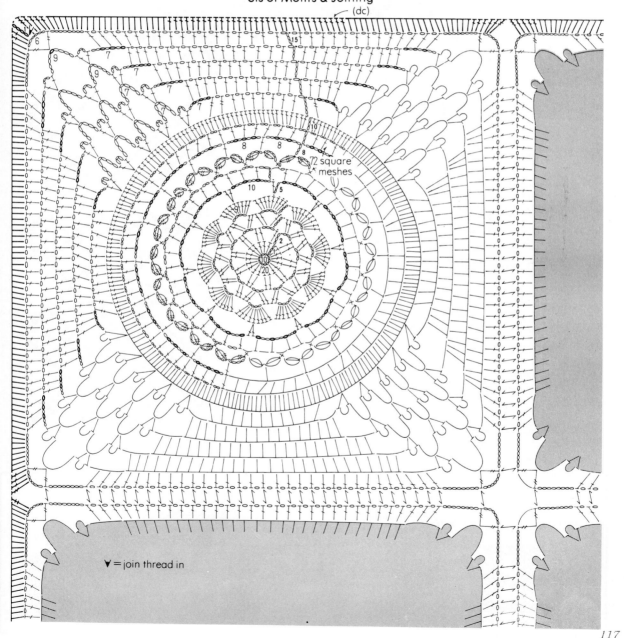

▼ = join thread in

117

From 2nd motif, work last row joining to previous motif.

Make 10 rows of 7 motifs. Work dc and tr along the edge all around.

Edging: Ch 121. Crochet patterns decreasing or increasing one side until 321 st row. From 322nd row, work decreasing each side. Go on to bottom edging. Work bottom side joining to the edge of side until 21st row. Work counter side in same manner.

Trimming: Row 1: Work sc on top side, alternate 1 sc, ch 3 on remaining sides.

Row 2: Work dc on top side, work "1 sc, ch 3, 3 dc in last sc" on remaining sides.

Having trimmed out-edge of edging, join to joined-motif working whip stitch along.

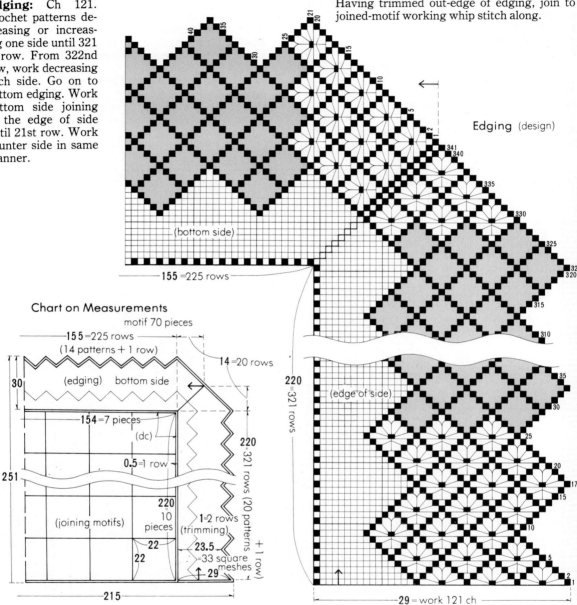

Edging (design)

Chart on Measurements

motif 70 pieces

Pattern St

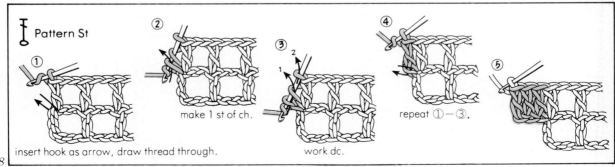

make 1 st of ch.

work dc.

repeat ①—③.

insert hook as arrow, draw thread through.

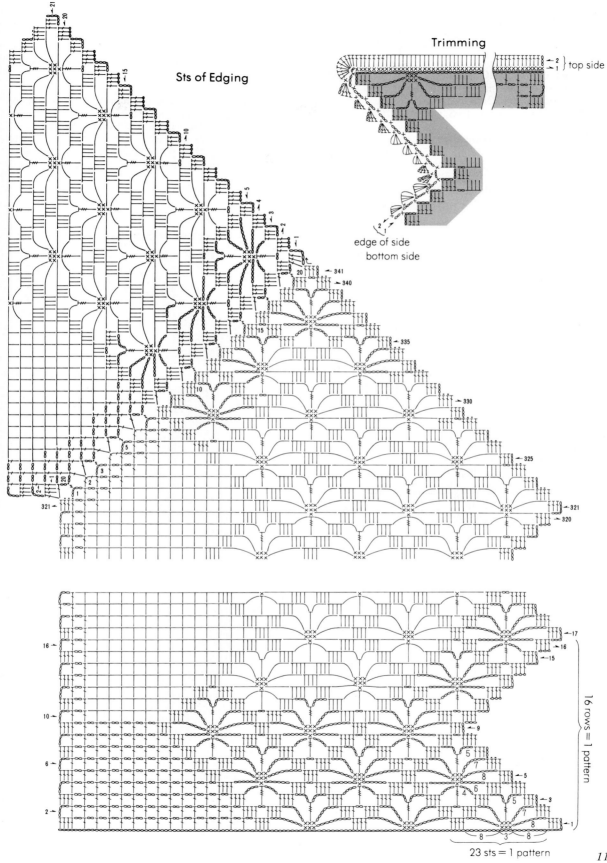

Sts of Edging

Trimming

} top side

edge of side
bottom side

16 rows = 1 pattern

23 sts = 1 pattern

24 Bedspread

shown on pages 46 - 47

You'll Need:
Crochet cotton DMC #15, 117 20-g. balls White.
Steel crochet hook size 1.00 mm.
Finished Size: 222 cm by 255.5 cm
Gauge: Filet crochet: 15.5 squares = 10 cm
18 rows = 10 cm
Making Instructions:
A-motif: Ch 127. Row 1: Ch 5, dc in 9th st from hook, (ch 2, sk 2 sts, 1 dc) 22 times, 18 dc, (ch 2, sk 2 sts, 1 dc) 13 times.
Row 2: Turn, ch 5, dc in dc, ch 2, dc in dc, continue in same way, working 2 dc instead of ch 2 for each bl.

Rows 3-429: Work straight in same manner, repeating 79 rows for each pattern.
Make 7 motifs.
B-motif: Ch 55. Work filet crochet increasing (or decreasing) one side as shown.
Make 2 pieces of 450 rows, 1 piece of 341 rows.
Finishing: Arrange motifs in position referring to chart, join together with whip stitch. Trim 3 sides working dc and sc along, finish top edge working 1 row of dc.

Inc or Dec on Side & Edge Trimming

Chart on Measurements

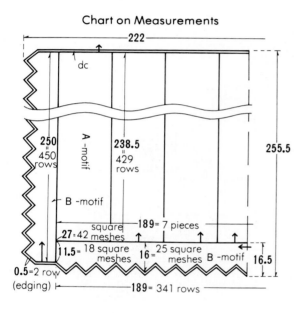

A-Motif

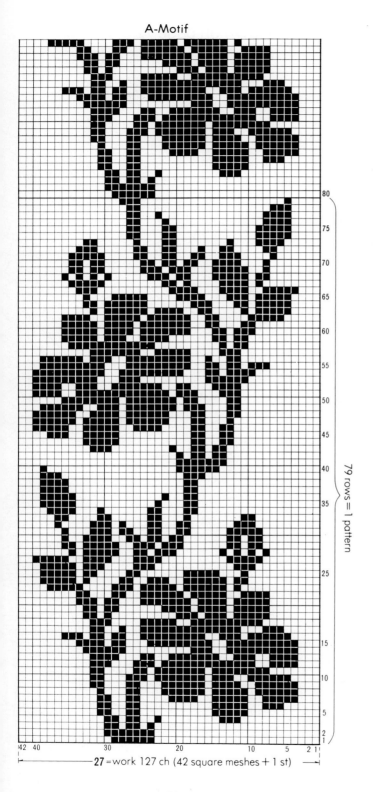

79 rows = 1 pattern

27 = work 127 ch (42 square meshes + 1 st)

B-Motif

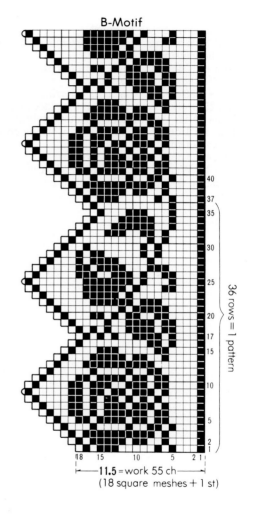

36 rows = 1 pattern

11.5 = work 55 ch
(18 square meshes + 1 st)

 =

38 Centerpiece shown on page 72

You'll Need:
Crochet cotton DMC #20, 3.5 20-g. balls White. Steel crochet hook size 0.90 mm.
Finished Size: 52 cm in diameter
Gauge: 1 row of dc = 0.6 cm
Making Instructions:
Ch 10, sl st in 1st ch to form ring.
Rnd 1: Ch 3, 23 dc in ring, sl st in 3rd st of beg ch.
Rnd 2: Dc in dc, ch 1, repeat.
Rnd 3: Work net st of ch-5 around, end working ch 3, 1 hdc, instead of ch 5.
Rnd 4: 3 dc in lp, ch 3, work "(1 sc, ch 4) 4 times, 1 sc" in next lp, ch 3, repeat.
Rnds 5-38: Make 6 patterns referring to chart. From rnd 25, work increasing sts at the place indicated.
Rnds 39-41: Work 1 dc, ch 2, alternately around.
Rnd 42: 1 dc, ch 3, repeat. End working ch 1, 1 hdc, instead of ch 3.
Rnd 43: 3 dc at a time, ch 2, repeat.
Rnd 44: Work 1 sc, ch 3, alternately around.
Finish in dodecagon. Care not to make sts of ch too firm.

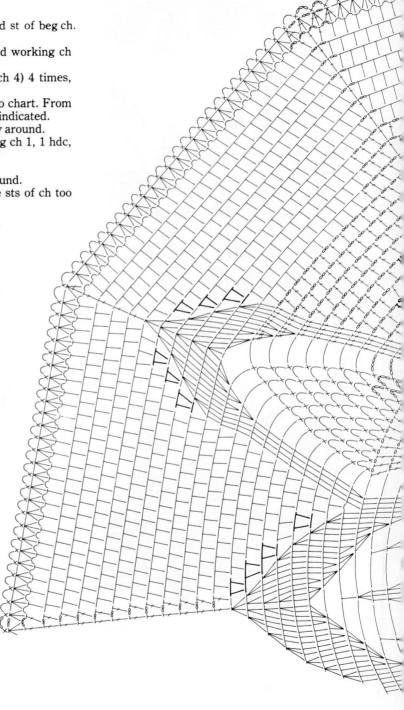

123

21 Bedspread

shown on pages 40 - 41

You'll Need:
Crochet cotton DMC #20, 141.5 20-g. balls White.
Steel crochet hook size 0.90 mm.
Finished Size: 247 cm by 281.5 cm
Size of Motif: Refer to chart.
Gauge: 1 row of dc = 0.5 cm
Making Instructions:
A-motif: Ch 10, sl st in 1st ch to form ring.
Row 1: Ch 1, 20 sc in ring, sl st in 1st ch.
Row 2: Ch 1, (1 sc, ch 2, 4-dc pop, ch 2) 10 times.
Row 3: Sl st in 3 sts, ch 3, 3 3-ch p, 1 dc, ch 2, * 1 dc, 3 3-ch p, 1 dc, ch 2, repeat from * around, sl st in 3rd st of beg ch. End off.
Row 4: Join cotton in middle p indicated, ch 3 (1 dc ch 10, sc in 4th st from the beg, dc in 1st st of beg ch, ch 5, continue in same manner around.

Row 5: Work 10 dc in each lp, 2 sc, ch 3, 2 sc, in each ch-5.
Row 6: * 1 sc, ch 3, 1 sc, ch 4, tr in ch-3 lp, ch 4, repeat from * around.
Row 7: Dc in each st around.
Rows 8-9: Alternate 1 dc, ch 3.
Row 10: Dc in each st around.
Rows 11-15: Work as for rows 8-10.
Rows 16-29: Join cotton in each of 4 patterns where indicated, work 1 pattern each turning each row at the end.
Trimming of A-motif: Row 1: Work sc and the ch of required sts alternately around.
Row 2: Work "1 sc, 1 hdc, 3 dc, 5-ch p, 3 dc, 1 hdc, 1 sc" in each lp around.
Make 71 pieces.
B-motif: Make half of A-motif referring to chart.
Make 26 pieces.

A-Motif

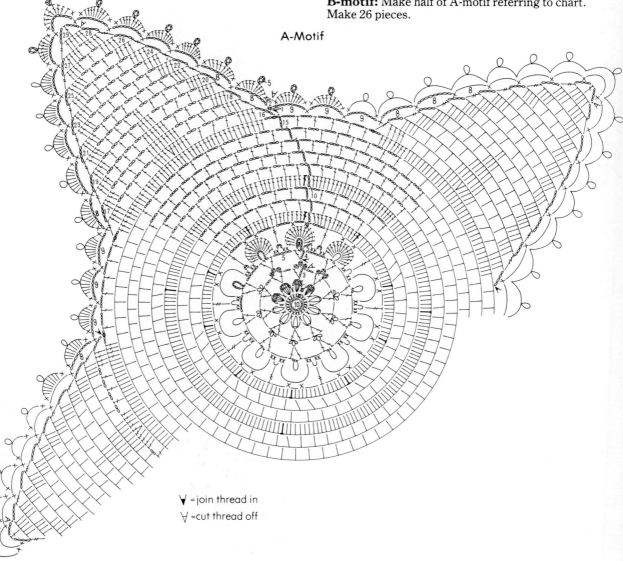

⋎ = join thread in
⋏ = cut thread off

Chart on Measurements

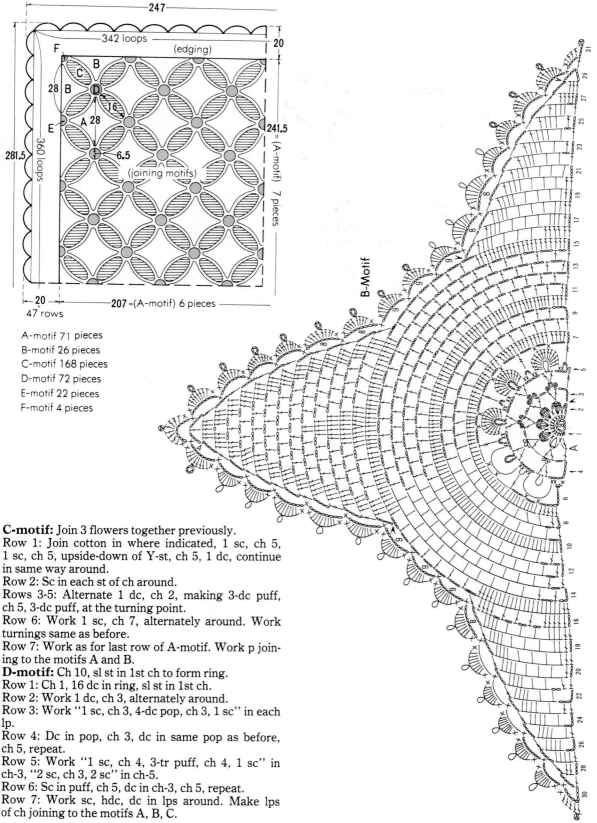

A-motif 71 pieces
B-motif 26 pieces
C-motif 168 pieces
D-motif 72 pieces
E-motif 22 pieces
F-motif 4 pieces

C-motif: Join 3 flowers together previously.
Row 1: Join cotton in where indicated, 1 sc, ch 5, 1 sc, ch 5, upside-down of Y-st, ch 5, 1 dc, continue in same way around.
Row 2: Sc in each st of ch around.
Rows 3-5: Alternate 1 dc, ch 2, making 3-dc puff, ch 5, 3-dc puff, at the turning point.
Row 6: Work 1 sc, ch 7, alternately around. Work turnings same as before.
Row 7: Work as for last row of A-motif. Work p joining to the motifs A and B.
D-motif: Ch 10, sl st in 1st ch to form ring.
Row 1: Ch 1, 16 dc in ring, sl st in 1st ch.
Row 2: Work 1 dc, ch 3, alternately around.
Row 3: Work "1 sc, ch 3, 4-dc pop, ch 3, 1 sc" in each lp.
Row 4: Dc in pop, ch 3, dc in same pop as before, ch 5, repeat.
Row 5: Work "1 sc, ch 4, 3-tr puff, ch 4, 1 sc" in ch-3, "2 sc, ch 3, 2 sc" in ch-5.
Row 6: Sc in puff, ch 5, dc in ch-3, ch 5, repeat.
Row 7: Work sc, hdc, dc in lps around. Make lps of ch joining to the motifs A, B, C.

125

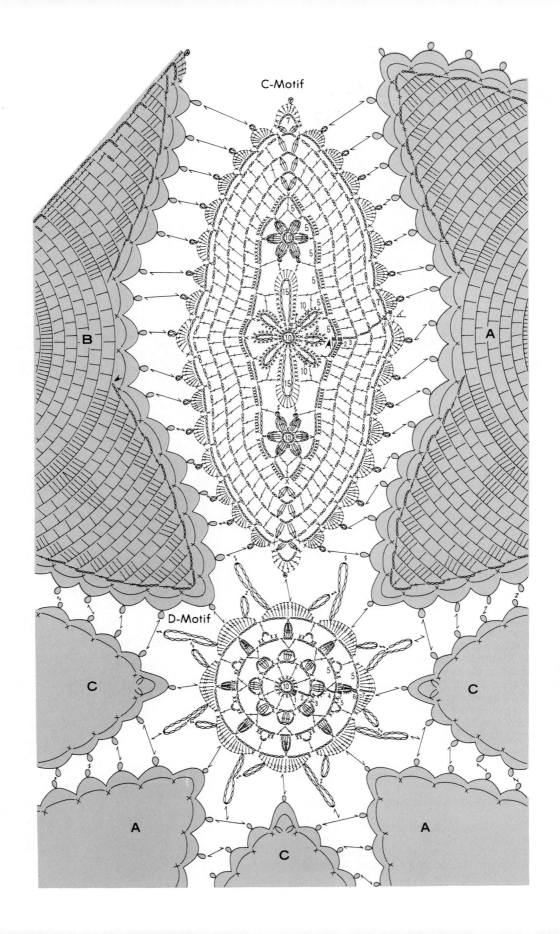

C-Motif

D-Motif

E-motif: Make half of D-motif. Join to the edge of joined-motif.

F-motif: Make quarter of D-motif, join in each of 4 corners.

Edging: Row 1: Work sc and ch around, making edges even.

Rows 2-11: Work dc on 3rd row, filet crochet of 1 dc, ch 2, for the rest. Inc at each corner referring to chart.

Row 12: Alternate 2 dc at a time and ch 8.

Row 13: Work "1 sc, 1 hdc, 3 dc, ch 2 (ch 3 each corner), 3 dc, 1 hdc, 1 sc" in each lp around.

Rows 14-16: Work pattern st as shown. When to work the sc on 16th row, wrap the lps of rows 14-15 together in the st.

Rows 17-25: Work as for rows 14-16.

Rows 26-37: Work referring to chart. End off.

Row 38: Net st of ch-6 around.

Rows 39-47: Complete 1 pattern each. Work crosswise following the arrows on the chart.

E-Motif

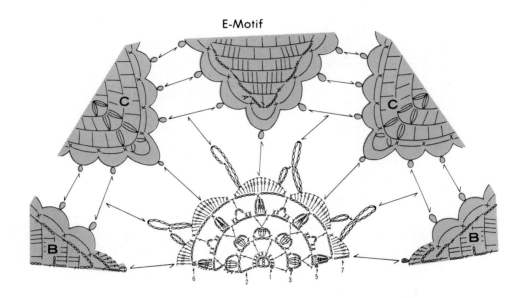

F-Motif

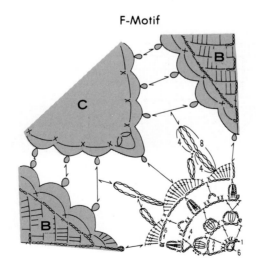

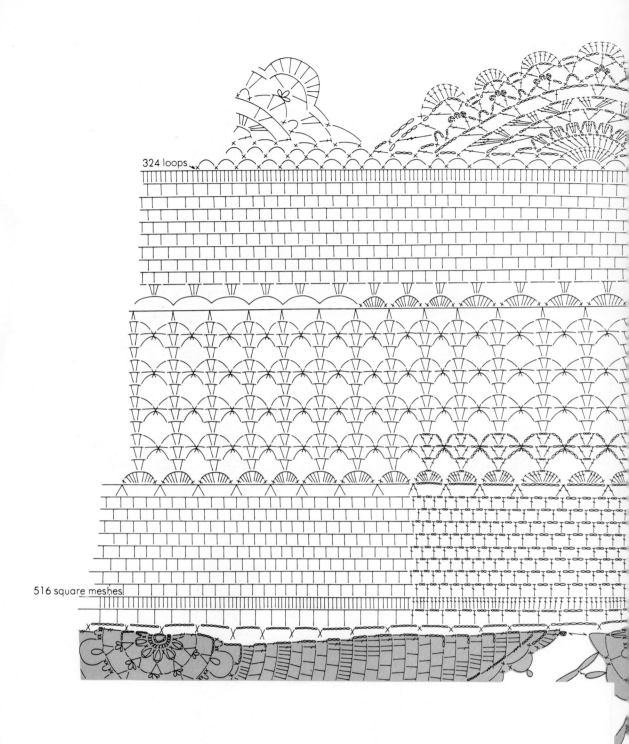

324 loops

516 square meshes

Edging

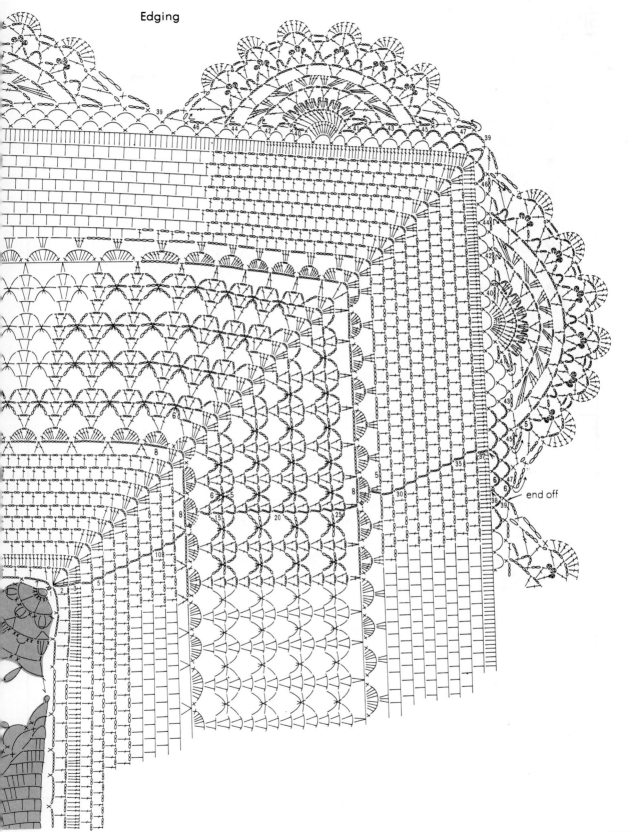

end off

SIGNS FOR STITCHES

chain stitch (ch)	single crochet (sc)	half double crochet (hdc)
double crochet (dc)	treble crochet (tr or trc)	double treble crochet (dtr)
triple treble crochet (tr tr)	sextuple treble crochet (str)	slip stitch (sl st)
2-single-crochet cluster (2-sc cluster)	3-single-crochet cluster (3-sc cluster)	2-single-crochet increase (2-sc inc.)
3-single-crochet increase (3-sc inc.)	3-double-crochet cluster (3-dc cluster)	3-double-crochet increase (3-dc inc.)
3-double-crochet puff (3-dc puff)	5-double-crochet popcorn (5-dc pop.)	3-chain picot (3-ch p)

Joining Motifs Together

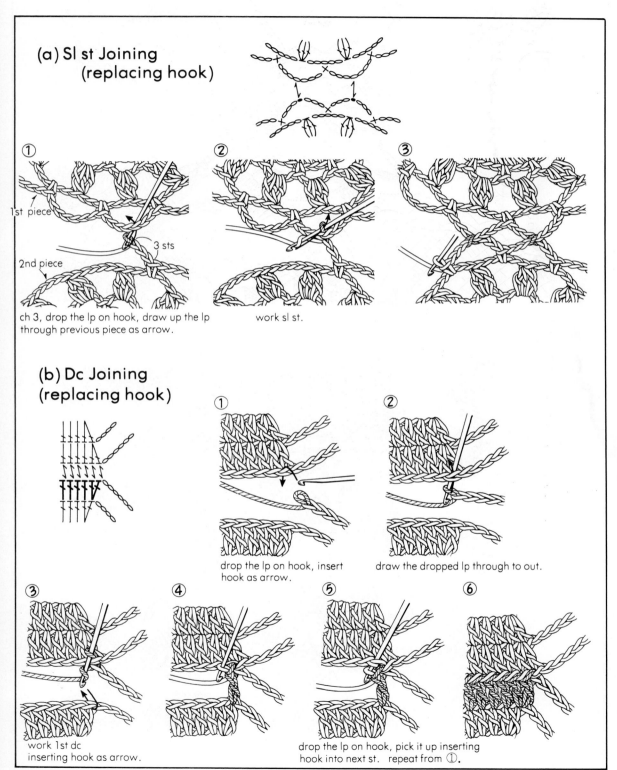

(a) Sl st Joining (replacing hook)

① 1st piece · 2nd piece · 3 sts

ch 3, drop the lp on hook, draw up the lp through previous piece as arrow.

② work sl st.

③

(b) Dc Joining (replacing hook)

① drop the lp on hook, insert hook as arrow.

② draw the dropped lp through to out.

③ work 1st dc inserting hook as arrow.

④

⑤ drop the lp on hook, pick it up inserting hook into next st. repeat from ①.

⑥

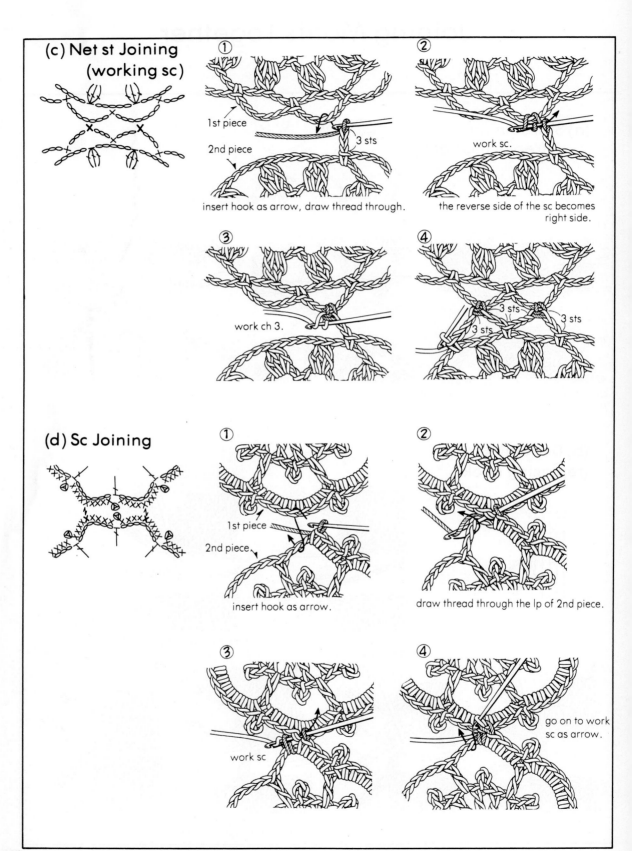

(c) Net st Joining (working sc)

① 1st piece
2nd piece
3 sts

insert hook as arrow, draw thread through.

② work sc.

the reverse side of the sc becomes right side.

③ work ch 3.

④ 3 sts
3 sts
3 sts

(d) Sc Joining

① 1st piece
2nd piece

insert hook as arrow.

② draw thread through the lp of 2nd piece.

③ work sc

④ go on to work sc as arrow.